Financial Education for Youth

THE ROLE OF SCHOOLS

BETTER POLICIES FOR BETTER LIVES

Please cite this publication as:
OECD (2014), Financial Education for Youth: The Role of Schools, OECD Publishing.
http://dx.doi.org/10.1787/9789264174825-en

ISBN 978-92-64-17481-8 (print)
ISBN 978-92-64-17482-5 (PDF)

Foreword

The importance of financial literacy and specifically the need to promote financial education has been recognised as an important contributor to improved financial inclusion and individuals' financial well-being as well as a support to financial stability. The relevance of financial education policies is acknowledged at the highest global policy level: in 2012, G20 Leaders endorsed the OECD/INFE High-level Principles on National Strategies for Financial Education that specifically identify youth as one of the priority targets of government policies in this domain. That same year, Asia-Pacific Economic Cooperation (APEC) Ministers of Finance identified financial literacy as a critical life skill.

This attention to financial education and in particular to youth is justified by the new challenges faced by youth globally, and by the greater financial competences that they require. Younger generations will face increasing financial risks, and will be confronted with more sophisticated financial products than did previous generations. They are now given access to financial services and products at an ever younger age. However, these developments do not appear to be matched by an equivalent increase in their financial skills. Evidence from national and OECD surveys shows that younger generations have lower levels of financial literacy compared with those of their parents, leading to potential new vulnerabilities. This mismatch potentially has important implications for example in terms of responsible use of credit, adequacy of saving for the long-term and retirement or even social, economic and financial inclusion of future generations.

Back in 2002, recognising the negative consequences of a lack of financial literacy, the OECD established a comprehensive project on financial education, under the aegis of the Committee on Financial Markets and the Insurance and Private Pensions Committee. In 2008, the OECD International Network on Financial Education (INFE), which now comprises 107 economies, was created to outreach beyond the OECD Member countries and strengthen information sharing, collect evidence, develop analytical work and related policy instruments. The focus on youth and on schools has been at the centre of the OECD and its INFE project since its inception. In 2005, the first OECD Recommendation on Principles and Good Practices for Financial Education and Awareness already acknowledged that "financial education should start at school. People should be educated about financial matters as early as possible in their lives".

Surveys conducted within the OECD/INFE since 2008 show that an increasing number of countries have implemented financial education programmes in schools. The surveys also point to the major challenges policy makers and interested stakeholders and practitioners face when they seek to introduce financial education in schools.

This publication, developed thanks to the support of the Russian Trust Fund for Financial Literacy and Education, analyses these challenges for the first time and provides interested policy makers and stakeholders with a framework to address youth's needs for financial education, efficient practices implemented in countries with diverse circumstances and education systems, a comparison of existing learning frameworks on financial education as well as guidance to effectively introduce financial education in schools.

The findings from this publication have been instrumental in the design of a financial literacy assessment for the first ever financial literacy option in the OECD Programme for International Student Assessment (PISA) in 2012. The publication of the results of the PISA Financial Literacy assessment in 2014 will, in turn, provide policy makers with essential empirical evidence on the levels of financial competencies of 15 years old students, which can be used to review, amend and expand existing practices.

The content of this publication was approved by the OECD/INFE and the OECD bodies in charge of financial education. It was welcomed by G20 Leaders in September 2013 as part of the Progress Report developed by the OECD on Youth and Finance.

ACKNOWLEDGMENTS

This publication is the result of a collaborative effort on the part of the OECD Secretariat and delegates to the OECD International Network on Financial Education (INFE). OECD/INFE delegates, and their counterparts within national administrations, helped preparing the first draft of the monograph and provided important inputs into the drafting of the Guidelines on Financial Education in Schools.

Though OECD/INFE delegates are too numerous to mention them all by name, their contribution to this book is gratefully acknowledged. The OECD would like to acknowledge in particular the contribution of the members of the OECD/INFE Expert Subgroup on Financial Education in Schools: Ms. Sue Lewis (Subgroup Leader), former HM Treasury, currently Financial Services Consumer Panel, United Kingdom; Ms. Delia Rickard, former Australian Securities and Investments Commission; Ms. Jane Rooney, Financial Consumer Agency of Canada; Ms. Ryoko Okazaki, Bank of Japan; Ms. Koid Swee Lian, Central Bank of Malaysia; Ms. Wilna Van Rossum, Dutch Ministry of Finance; Ms. Diana Crossan, former Financial Literacy and Retirement Income Commission of New Zealand; Mr. Michal Nalepa, Polish Financial Supervision Authority; Mr. Andrei Markov, The World Bank; Ms. Olivia Davids, former Financial Services Board of South Africa. A special thank goes to Dr. Susan Watson, Education Consultant, who contributed to the preparation of early drafts of parts of the publication.

The OECD would also like to acknowledge the contribution of the members of the PISA Financial Literacy Expert Group, whose work was instrumental in developing the PISA Financial Literacy Framework that provided useful inputs for the preparation of Chapter 1. These are Mr. Jean-Pierre Boisivon, Université de Paris II Panthéon-Assas, France; Ms. Diana Crossan, former Retirement Commission, New Zealand; Mr. Peter Cuzner, Australian Securities and Investments Commission; Ms. Jeanne Hogarth, former Federal Reserve System, United States; Mr. Dušan Hradil, Ministry of Finance, Czech Republic; Mr. Stan Jones, consultant, Canada; Ms. Sue Lewis, former HM Treasury, United Kingdom; Prof. Annamaria Lusardi, Dartmouth College and The George Washington University School of Business, United States.

Finally, the OECD would like to acknowledge the inputs received by the International and Curriculum Policy Division of the United Kingdom Department for Education as well as the Financial Capability team within the United Kingdom HM Treasury; Ms. Tracey Bleakley, Personal Finance Education Group (pfeg), United Kingdom; Ms. Judy Gordon, Australian Securities and Investments Commission; the Dutch Institute for Family Finance Information (Nibud); and the Ministry of Education of New Zealand.

The publication was prepared under the direction of Ms. Flore-Anne Messy, manager of the financial education project and Secretary of the INFE, and by Mr. Andrea Grifoni, Policy Analyst within the Financial Affairs Division, with technical support from Mr. Edward Smiley.

The research for this book was conducted as part of the programme of work of the OECD's financial education project, which has been supported by the Russian/World Bank/OECD Trust Fund on Financial Literacy and Education.

Table of contents

Executive summary

Most national financial education[1] strategies have youth among the key target groups. As such, they aim at introducing financial education into the school curriculum and designing dedicated learning frameworks. The rationale for this focus and these new policy endeavours is multi-fold. First, while financial education concerns all ages, the education of younger generations on financial issues has become all the more important since they will likely bear more financial risks and be faced with increasingly complex and sophisticated financial products than their parents. Second, the young have access to, and are being offered, financial services at ever earlier ages (through pocket money, mobile phones, bank accounts, or even credit cards). Yet, most recent surveys show worrying low levels of youth financial literacy and, in many cases, significantly lower levels than older generations.

Against this backdrop, effective practices and results of existing programmes' evaluation show that including financial education in the formal school curriculum is one of the most efficient and fair ways to reach a whole generation on a broad scale. In addition, since the curriculum spans several years and can start as early as kindergarten, it is a unique means to inculcate and nurture a sound financial culture and behaviours amongst future adults. This is especially important since parents are unequally equipped to transmit to their children sound financial habits. Besides, as demonstrated in other related education fields (such as health), young people are potentially good disseminators of new habits in the rest of the population.

Yet the successful integration of financial education in school curricula can be challenging in many respects owing to a vast range of constraints, notably due to the fact that this is a new endeavour for most national administrations. These challenges include: lack of resources and time; overloaded curricula; insufficient expertise and know how; lack of easily available high quality materials; the variety of stakeholders involved; limited political willingness and commitment.

To address these challenges, the OECD International Network on Financial Education (INFE), with the support of the Russian Trust Fund on Financial Literacy and Financial Education, decided to develop research and guidelines to support the introduction and implementation of financial education in schools where needed. This work has been conducted through a dedicated group of experts and built on preliminary surveys conducted by the OECD Committee on Financial Markets in 2008, broad data collection conducted through the OECD/INFE in 2008/2013, as well as further research and analytical work prepared by the OECD/INFE and the OECD Secretariat.

The publication is a compendium of this extensive work and surveys. It provides policy makers with the rationale and framework for addressing the financial education needs of youth, a review of the main challenges and case studies of good practices as well as INFE Guidelines to successfully introduce financial education in schools.

Chapter 1 highlights the importance of financial literacy in the context of the global trends affecting both the risks borne by individuals and the changes in the demand and supply of financial services. It addresses specifically the need to focus on youth, and the rationale for doing so through schools.

Chapter 2 presents the main issues to be taken into consideration when introducing financial education in schools, and specific case studies showing the ways in which countries with different institutional frameworks and uneven resources have addressed similar challenges. These selected relevant experiences support the implementation of the Guidelines presented in Annex and assist countries in the design and implementation of financial education programmes in schools.

The topics of the case studies were identified by the OECD/INFE due to their importance and their relevance to policy makers. They include crucial elements such as political support to make financial education in school effective and sustainable over time, modalities of its introduction in schools, the training needed for teachers, the tools and pedagogical materials, the role of resources as well as the importance of programme evaluation.

Finally, chapter 3 provides a comparative analysis of existing learning frameworks for the formal school sector in Australia, Brazil, England, Japan, Malaysia, The Netherlands, New Zealand, Northern Ireland, Scotland, South Africa and the United States. These are followed by detailed examples of learning outcomes and standards for financial education, at the primary or secondary level. The chapter is articulated around two sections. The first one provides a comparative analysis of existing learning frameworks in relation to their institutional and organisational development, their content and pedagogical features. The second section presents frameworks in relation to their key characteristics.

The selected experiences clarify the history of the development of the frameworks, putting them in a broader context that includes national strategies for financial education and analysing the role played by key institutions in initiating such programmes. They provide further details over the learning outcomes and the topics and objectives addressed in different school grades.

The INFE Guidelines for Financial Education in Schools and the guidance on learning frameworks are included in Annex A. They address the main steps for the introduction of financial education into schools and provide guidance on the development of a consistent and sustainable framework for its integration in school programmes. A successful introduction is better achieved through the setting of quantifiable and appropriate goals, matched by flexible modalities of introduction. It should also take into account resources and plan impact monitoring and evaluation. The Guidelines also highlight the need to ensure a suitable level of involvement of public authorities and educational system, teachers and parents, and other important stakeholders such as the private sector and NGOs. The Guidelines also stress the importance of the design and promotion of efficient means and incentives, methods for training teachers, the provision of adequate pedagogical material, and assessment of students' competencies.

The Annex includes guidance on the design of an appropriate learning framework for financial education, introducing topics that are addressed in more detail through concrete examples in chapter 3. The focus of the guidance is on the purpose of the framework, the outcomes that students are expected to develop, and on characteristics such as length of courses and specific content, pedagogical tools, assessment of students' results, monitoring and evaluation.

Note

1. The term "financial education" in a school context is used to refer to the teaching of financial knowledge, understanding, skills, behaviours, attitudes and values which will enable students to make savvy and effective financial decisions in their daily life and when they become adults. The outcome of financial education is typically referred to as financial literacy or financial capability. For the sake of clarity and consistency with OECD/INFE terminology, in this publication the term "financial literacy" will be used except when referring to programmes or documents developed by countries that use a different terminology. Financial literacy, as defined for young people within the OECD PISA Financial Literacy Framework, is "knowledge and understanding of financial concepts and risks, and the skills, motivation and confidence to apply such knowledge and understanding in order to make effective decisions across a range of financial contexts, to improve the financial well-being of individuals and society, and to enable participation in economic life".

Chapter 1

The importance of financial education for youth

This chapter presents the global trends underpinning the rising importance of financial literacy, from improved financial inclusion and innovation to the transfer of (financial) risks to individuals. It then highlights the benefits of financial literacy for individuals, and its positive spillovers on the financial and economic system. The chapter also points to the rationale for a focus on youth and in particular on schools. It notably draws on OECD/INFE surveys, desk research and work developed for the preparation of the OECD PISA Financial Literacy Framework.

The importance of financial literacy for individuals

In recent years, advanced and emerging economies have become increasingly concerned about the level of financial literacy of their citizens. This has stemmed in particular from improved levels of financial inclusion and rising middle classes in emerging economies, as well as wide-ranging developments in the financial marketplace, shrinking public and private support systems, and shifting demographic profiles including the ageing of the population. Concern was also heightened by the financial crisis, with the recognition that lack of financial literacy was one of the factors contributing to bad financial decisions and that these decisions could, in turn, have tremendous negative spill-overs (INFE/OECD, 2009; OECD, 2009a; see also Gerardi, Goette, and Meier, 2010 for empirical analysis of financial literacy and mortgage delinquency).

As a result, financial literacy is now globally acknowledged as an important element of economic and financial stability and development. In 2012 and 2013, G20 leaders notably endorsed the OECD/INFE High-level Principles on National Strategies for Financial Education, recognised the importance of financial education for youth and called for the identification of potential barriers faced by youth in their access to financial products and financial education, and welcomed Progress Reports on Youth and Finance developed by the OECD on financial education and by the World Bank on financial inclusion (G20 Leaders communiqué, 2012; G20 Leaders communiqué, 2013). This attention is justified by a series of tangible trends (OECD, 2005a), which make financial literacy a key life skill for individuals. This includes Asia-Pacific Economic Cooperation Ministers of Finance who recognised *the importance of financial literacy as a critical life skill in the 21st century that can contribute to individual and families' wellbeing as well as to financial stability in our economies."* (APEC Policy Statement, August 2012)

The following sections present these trends, highlight the benefits of financial education and the importance of its introduction in schools.

Greater supply of a wide range of financial products and services

In most countries, growing numbers of consumers have now access to a wide range of financial products and services, from a variety of providers and delivered through various channels. Improved levels of financial inclusion in emerging economies, developments in technology and deregulation have resulted in widening access to retail financial products, from current accounts to remittances products, consumer revolving credit and equity portfolios. The products available are also becoming more complex, and individuals are required to make comparisons across a number of factors such as the fees charged, interest rates paid or received, length of contract and exposure to risk. They must also identify appropriate providers and delivery channels from the vast array of possibilities, including community groups, traditional financial institutions, online banks and mobile phone companies.

Increased demand for financial products and services

Economic and technological developments have also brought greater global connectedness and massive changes in communications and financial transactions, as well as in social interactions and consumer behaviour. Such changes have made it more important that individuals be able to interact with financial providers. In particular, consumers often need access to financial services (including banks and other providers such as Post Offices) in order to make and receive electronic payments like income, remittances and online transactions, as well as to conduct face-to-face transactions in societies where cash and cheques are no longer favoured. Those who cannot access such services often pay more for cash transactions, using informal financial services such as moneylenders or cheque cashers (Kempson, Collard, and Moore, 2005).

Risk shift

In parallel, there has been a widespread transfer of risk from both governments and employers to individuals. Many governments are reducing or have reduced state-supported pensions, and some are reducing healthcare benefits. Defined contribution pension plans are quickly replacing defined benefit pension plans, shifting onto workers the responsibility to save for their own financial security after retirement. Traditional pay-as-you-go (PAYG) pension schemes are supplemented by new schemes in which the individual is subject to both revenue and investment risks. Most surveys show that a majority of workers are unaware of the risks they now have to face, and do not have sufficient knowledge and skill to manage such risks adequately, even if they are aware of them (OECD, 2008). Furthermore, the array of demographic and financial risks that people have to face is increasing: and notably the risks associated with longevity and health, credit, financial markets volatility, as well as unemployment.

Increased individual responsibility

The number of financial decisions that individuals have to make is increasing as a consequence of changes in the market and the economy. For instance, longer life expectancy means individuals need to ensure that they accumulate savings to cover much longer periods of retirement. People also need to assume more responsibility for funding personal or family healthcare needs. Moreover, increasing education costs make it important for parents to plan and invest adequately for their children's education. Even when individuals use the services of financial intermediaries and advisors, they need to understand what is being offered or advised. The individual is responsible for the financial product he or she decides to purchase, and the individual will face all the consequences of the choice. In addition, the current economic and financial environment can make it even more difficult for individuals to find and remain in a stable and salaried occupation.

All of these trends have transferred the responsibility of major financial decisions to individuals. At the same time, they have both enlarged the options for the majority of the population (including new financial consumers) and increased the level of complexity they face. Against this backdrop, individuals are expected to be sufficiently financially literate and entrepreneurial to take the necessary steps to protect themselves and their relatives and ensure their financial well-being including by coping with unexpected events and/or developing their own source of income.

Benefits of financial literacy

Existing empirical evidence shows that adults in both developed and emerging economies who have been exposed to financial education are subsequently more likely than others to save and plan for retirement (Bernheim, Garrett, and Maki, 2001; Cole, Sampson, and Zia, 2010; Lusardi, 2009). This evidence suggests a link between financial education and outcomes; it indicates that improved levels of financial literacy can lead to positive behavioural change.

Other research, stemming largely from developed countries, and the United States in particular, indicates a number of potential benefits of being financially literate. There is mounting evidence that those with higher financial literacy are better able to manage their money, participate in the stock market and perform better on their portfolio choice, and that they are more likely to choose mutual funds with lower fees (Hastings and Tejeda-Ashton, 2008; Hilgert, Hogarth, and Beverly, 2003; Lusardi and Mitchell, 2008; Lusardi and Mitchell, 2011; Stango and Zinman, 2009; van Rooij, Lusardi, and Alessie, 2011; Yoong, 2011). Moreover, those who have greater financial knowledge are more likely to accumulate higher amounts of wealth (Lusardi and Mitchell, 2011).

Higher levels of financial literacy have been found to be related not only to asset building but also to credit and debt management, with more financially literate individuals opting for less costly mortgages and avoiding high interest payments and additional fees (Gerardi, et al., 2010; Lusardi and Tufano, 2009a, 2009b; Moore, 2003).

In addition to the benefits identified for individuals, financial literacy is important to economic and financial stability for a number of reasons. Financially literate consumers can make more informed decisions and demand higher quality services, which will encourage competition and innovation in the market. They are also less likely to react to market conditions in unpredictable ways, less likely to make unfounded complaints and more likely to take appropriate steps to manage the risks transferred to them. All of these factors will lead to a more efficient financial services sector and potentially less costly financial regulatory and supervisory requirements. They can also ultimately help in reducing government aid (and taxation) aimed at assisting those who have taken unwise financial decisions – or no decision at all.

Financial education for youth and in schools

In this context, the focus on financial education for youth and in schools is not new. As mentioned, financial literacy is increasingly considered to be an essential life skill including by regional and global fora such as G20 and APEC (G20, 2012; APEC 2012). In fact, as early as 2005, the OECD Recommendation advised that "financial education should start at school. People should be educated about financial matters as early as possible in their lives" (OECD, 2005b). Two main reasons underpin this recommendation: the importance of focusing on youth, and the efficiency of providing financial education in schools.

Focus on youth

Owing notably to technological advances, younger generations are likely to be more financially included in their adulthood than older generations and to use financial services to perform a wider array of activities throughout their lives. They will also probably have to bear more financial risks in adulthood than their parents. In particular, they are likely to be responsible for the planning of their own retirement savings and investments, and the coverage of their healthcare needs. They may also have to deal with increasingly sophisticated and innovative financial products, services and markets.

In a growing range of countries, youth have access to financial services from a young age. It is not uncommon for them to have accounts with access to online payment facilities or to use mobile phones (with various payment options) even before they become teenagers. Before leaving school, they may also face decisions about such issues as car insurance, savings products and overdrafts. Furthermore, the development of appropriate financial skills can also boost entrepreneurship and provide youth with additional tools in case they will experience economic hardship.

Given the complexities of new financial systems and their constant evolution, as well as social welfare systems (and particularly pension systems) and demographic trends, current generations are unlikely to be able to learn from past generations. Youth will have to rely on their own financial literacy[1] including not only knowledge, but more importantly sound competencies and new habits and attitudes to make savvy financial decisions and informed use of professional financial advice where they exist. However, surveys conducted nationally and globally show that young adults display lower levels of financial literacy compared to older generations (Atkinson and Messy, 2012 and Kempson, E., V. Perotti P., K. Scott, 2013).

These new and evolving competencies will thus have to be acquired through an ongoing process throughout individuals' lives. To be effective and lead to behavioural changes, this process has to start early in life (OECD, 2005). In fact, research and surveys conducted in various countries including Australia, the United Kingdom and the United States (see Whitebread and Bingham, 2013, for a review of the literature) show that the development and integration of financial habits and attitudes begin very early and probably before children reach seven years old.

It is also important that youth be financially literate before they engage in major financial transactions and contracts. In many countries, at around the age of 15 to 18, young people (and their parents) face one of their most important financial decisions: that is, whether or not to invest in college or higher education. The gap in wages between college and non-college educated workers has widened in many economies. At the same time, the education costs borne by students and their families have increased, often leading to an excessive reliance on credit (Smithers, 2010; Bradley, 2012; Ratcliffe and McKernan, 2013).

Finally, efforts to improve financial literacy in adulthood through the workplace or other settings can be severely limited by a lack of early exposure to financial education. It is therefore important to provide early opportunities to establish the foundations of financial literacy.

Efficiency of providing financial education in schools

When addressing young people's needs for greater financial competencies, the role of schools is paramount.

Research suggests that there is a link between financial literacy and family economic as well as educational background: those who are more financially literate disproportionately come from highly educated and financially sophisticated families (Lusardi, Mitchell, and Curto, 2010; Atkinson and Messy, 2012). In order to provide equality of opportunity, it is important to offer financial education to those who would not otherwise have access to it. Schools are well positioned to advance financial literacy among all demographic groups (including vulnerable groups such as low income and/or migrants families) within a generation, which will help to break the cycle of generational financial illiteracy. Schools also have the potential to reach out to parents, teachers and to disseminate sound financial habits in the wider community.

Moreover, school provides a relevant context to develop high quality teaching and effective learning. Existing curricula, pedagogical tools and school resources can indeed be harnessed to address youth's needs for financial education. Children in the school context are also a particularly appropriate audience with the necessary time and ability to learn. The country case studies of effective practices presented in the following chapters as well as the results of impact assessments notably conducted in Brazil (Bruhn, M., et al 2013, forthcoming) demonstrate that the introduction of financial education is effective when delivered in an engaging and consistent way (Lührmann et al., 2012).

Recognising both the importance of financial literacy for youth and the unique potential of school programmes, an increasing number of countries started delivering financial education in schools. OECD/INFE ongoing surveys reveal that over 40 countries have introduced some form of financial education in schools. These initiatives are developed at national, regional and local levels and also include pilot exercises. A shorter but constantly evolving list of countries have introduced financial education as a compulsory subject in schools generally through a cross-curricular approach.

Most countries however highlight that the introduction of financial education in schools is challenging for a series of reasons, including limited political willingness, and commitment; overloaded curricula; insufficient expertise and know how; lack of high quality materials; lack of resources and time; as well as the variety of stakeholders involved.

Against this backdrop, the following Chapter (2) sketches out the experience of countries which have overcome these challenges through strategies to secure the support of government and public authorities, and flexible but consistent approaches to the introduction of financial education into schools. It also highlights tools to support the provision of financial education in schools (including the training of teachers and the development of good pedagogic materials); and to ensure the sustainability of the programmes (including earmarking of resources and evaluation of programmes). Chapter 3 then addresses the content of learning frameworks developed for financial education in schools. Finally, the INFE Guidelines for Financial Education in Schools displayed in Annex A provide policy makers and interested stakeholders with high-level international guidance on the introduction of financial education in schools and guidance on the development of adapted learning frameworks.

Note

1. See Definition of financial literacy for 15 year old students, OECD (2013a), "Financial Literacy Framework": Financial literacy is knowledge and understanding of financial concepts and risks, and the skills, motivation and confidence to apply such knowledge and understanding in order to make effective decisions across a range of financial contexts, to improve the financial well-being of individuals and society, and to enable participation in economic life.

References

APEC (2012), Finance Ministers Joint Policy Statement. http://www.apec.org/Meeting-Papers/Ministerial-Statements/Finance/2012_finance.aspx

Atkinson, A., and Messy, F. (2012). Measuring Financial Literacy: Results of the OECD / International Network on Financial Education (INFE) Pilot Study. In OECD (Ed.), *OECD Working Papers on Finance, Insurance and Private Pensions* (Vol. 15): OECD Publishing.

Bernheim, D., Garrett, D., and Maki, D. (2001). Education and saving: The long-term effects of high school financial curriculum mandates. Journal of Public Economics, 85, 435-565.

Bradley, L. (2012), *Young People and Savings*. Institute for Public Policy Research, London.

Bruhn, M., B. Zia, A. Legovini and R. Marchetti (2014, forthcoming), "Financial Literacy for High School Students and Their Parents: Evidence from Brazil", World Bank.

Cole, S., Sampson, T., and Zia, B. (2010). Prices or Knowledge? What Drives Demand for Financial Services in Emerging Markets? HBS Working Papers 09-11, forthcoming in *The Journal of Finance*.

G20 (2012), Leaders Declaration, June.
www.g20mexico.org/images/stories/docs/g20/conclu/G20_Leaders_Declaration_2012.pdf

G20 (2013), Leaders Declaration, September, http://www.g20.org/load/782795034

Gerardi, K., Goette, L., and Meier, S. (2010). Financial Literacy and Subprime Mortgage Delinquency: Evidence from a Survey Matched to Administrative Data. *Federal Reserve Bank of Atlanta, 2010-10*.

Hastings, J., and Tejeda-Ashton, L. (2008). Financial Literacy, Information, and Demand Elasticity: Survey and Experimental Evidence from Mexico. *NBER Working Paper, 14538*.

Hilgert, M. A., Hogarth, J. M., and Beverly, S. G. (2003). Household Financial Management: The Connection Between Knowledge and Behavior. *Federal Reserve Bulletin, 89*(7), 309-322.

Kempson, E., Collard, S., and Moore, N. (2005). *Measuring financial capability: an exploratory study*. London: Financial Services Authority.

Kempson, E., V. Perotti P., K. Scott (2013) *Measuring financial capability: a new instrument and results from low- and middle-income countries*. International Bank for Reconstruction and Development / The World Bank, Washington, DC.

Lührmann M., M. Serra-Garcia and J. Winter, (2012), "The effects of financial literacy training: Evidence from a field experiment with German high-school children", University of Munich Discussion Paper No. 2012-24, http://epub.ub.uni-muenchen.de/14101/

Lusardi, A. (2009). U.S. Household Savings Behavior: The Role of Financial Literacy, Information and Financial Education Programs. In C. Foote, L. Goette and S. Meier (Eds.), *Policymaking Insights from Behavioral Economics* (pp. 109-149): Federal Reserve Bank of Boston.

Lusardi, A., and Mitchell, O. S. (2011). Financial Literacy and Planning: Implications for Retirement Wellbeing. In A. Lusardi and O. S. Mitchell (Eds.), *Financial Literacy: Implications for Retirement Security and the Financial Marketplace*: Oxford University Press.

Lusardi, A., Mitchell, O. S., and Curto, V. (2010). Financial literacy among the young. *The Journal of Consumer Affairs, 44*(2), 358-380.

Lusardi, A., and Tufano, P. (2009a). Debt Literacy, Financial Experiences, and Overindebtedness. NBER Working Paper n. 14808.

Lusardi, A., and Tufano, P. (2009b). Teach Workers about the Perils of Debt. *Harvard Business Review* (November), 22-24.

Moore, D. (2003). *Survey of Financial Literacy in Washington State: Knowledge, Behavior, Attitudes, and Experiences*: Social and Economic Sciences Research Center, Washington State University.

OECD (2005a), *Improving Financial Literacy: Analysis of Issues and Policies*, OECD Publishing. doi: 10.1787/9789264012578-en

OECD (2005b). *Recommendation on Principles and Good Practices for Financial Education and Awareness*: OECD, Directorate for Financial and Enterprise Affairs, http://www.oecd.org/finance/financial-education/35108560.pdf

OECD (2008), *Improving Financial Education and Awareness on Insurance and Private Pensions*, OECD Publishing. doi: 10.1787/9789264046399-en

OECD. (2009a). Financial Literacy and Consumer Protection: Overlooked Aspects of the Crisis. from http://www.financial-education.org/dataoecd/32/3/43138294.pdf

OECD/INFE. (2009b), Financial Education and the Crisis: Policy Paper and Guidance. June 2009. www.oecd.org/finance/financial-education/50264221.pdf

OECD (2013), "Financial Literacy Framework", in OECD, *PISA 2012 Assessment and Analytical Framework: Mathematics, Reading, Science, Problem Solving and Financial Literacy*, OECD Publishing.
doi: 10.1787/9789264190511-7-en

Ratcliffe C., S. McKernan (2013), Forever in Your Debt: Who Has Student Loan Debt, and Who's Worried. The Urban Institute and FINRA Investor Education Foundation.

Sherraden S. M., Johnson L., Guo B., Elliot W. (2010). Financial capability in children: Effects of participation in school-based financial education and savings program. *Journal of Family and Economic Issues, 32*, 385–399.
doi: 10.1007/s10834-010-9220-5

Smithers, R. (2010, 18 March 2010).
http://www.guardian.co.uk/money/2010/mar/18/university-students-graduate-mouting-debts. *Guardian*.

Van Rooij, M. A., Lusardi, A., and Alessie, R. (2011). Financial Literacy and Stock Market Participation. *Journal of Financial Economics, 101*(2), 449-472.

Whitebread, David and Sue Bingham (2013), *Habit Formation and Learning in Young Children*, Money Advice Service, London.
https://www.moneyadviceservice.org.uk/files/the-money-advice-service-habit-formation-and-learning-in-young-children-may2013.pdf

Yoong, J. (2011). Financial Illiteracy and Stock Market Participation: Evidence from the RAND American Life Panel. In A. Lusardi and O. S. Mitchell (Eds.), *Financial Literacy: Implications for Retirement Security and the Financial Marketplace*: Oxford University Press.

Chapter 2

Implementing financial education in schools

This chapter addresses the most challenging implementation aspects of the introduction of financial education in schools and illustrates the INFE Guidelines for Financial Education in Schools presented in Annex A. It provides policy makers with selected relevant experiences and effective practices from countries that developed or are currently developing financial education programmes in schools. The chapter provides examples of initial steps, such as securing the support of government and public authorities, and effective ways of introducing financial education into schools, showing examples of cross-curricular or – more rarely - stand-alone approaches. It then addresses the provision of financial education programmes, from the training of teachers to the development of good pedagogic materials. It finally highlights ways to reinforce the sustainability of programmes through partnerships with the private sector and evaluation of programmes. These examples aim to assist in the design and implementation of financial education in schools by showing how different countries addressed the same issues in different ways given their peculiar institutional asset, educational framework, funding component and political support for the introduction of these programmes.

The case study topics were selected by the OECD International Network on Financial Education (INFE) due to their importance for the successful introduction and implementation of financial education programmes. The OECD/INFE conducted ongoing surveys from 2008 to 2013 to identify experiences that related directly to these case study topics.

Strategies to promote and influence political willingness

The development and implementation of financial education programmes in schools need the involvement of several stakeholders with diverse backgrounds. In this respect, it is important that the government and the relevant public authorities take a leading and coordinating role.

As established by the OECD/INFE High-level Principles on National Strategies for Financial Education (OECD/INFE, 2012), public authorities are best placed to provide effective leadership at the national level and ensure the sustainability and the credibility of the programme (see also Grifoni and Messy, 2012; Russia's G20 Presidency – OECD, 2013). They also have the tools and the means to plan and implement effective communication strategies aimed at convincing policy and educational decision-makers of the importance of financial education. They can find ways to effectively incorporate financial education into school curricula and assess which tools are available to support effective practice. Finally, public authorities are well equipped to understand the context in which financial education programmes can contribute to the achievement of the requirements of school curricula, and are essential in ensuring the involvement of all the other relevant stakeholders.

However, most countries face difficulties in convincing policy makers and especially the educational system of the importance of introducing financial education in schools.

Following the INFE Guidelines presented in Annex A, the five selected cases sketched out hereinafter (Australia, Brazil, New Zealand, South Africa and the United Kingdom) provide different yet successful experience in influencing political willingness in order to incorporate financial education into school curricula.

The Australian approach to securing the inclusion of financial literacy in school curricula has been based on the use of formal educational approaches and on the establishment of cooperative partnerships. In 2008, the national financial regulator -the Australian Securities Investment Commission (ASIC) – took over the lead responsibility for advancing financial education in schools. This role was previously undertaken by a the Financial Literacy Foundation, which was established in 2005 by the Australian Government within the Department of Treasury to raise awareness of consumer issues and encourage all Australians to better manage their money.

Brazil offers a good example of financial education in schools addressed as the first priority of its national strategy. This allowed for a structured co-operation among stakeholders from both educational and financial authorities, and for the creation of dedicated institutional mechanisms within the national strategy structure. Furthermore, the Brazilian approach has been informed by the need to foster dialogue in the context of a federal state.

The New Zealand case demonstrates the importance of baseline surveys in providing quality data for policy makers, of the role played by a strong and defined leadership by one institution and of the value of strategic partnership with the Ministry of Education and nation-wide private financial institutions. The initial survey that portrayed low levels of financial literacy among the population provided an opportunity for a high-level public sector body to lead the partnership with the private sector, ensuring its control by the appointment of a Board of senior government officials that overlooked most aspects of the National Strategy.

South Africa is also a good example. In the absence of an implemented national strategy (at that time) but in the context of a general mandate on the promotion of informational and educational programmes related to the use of financial products, stakeholders were encouraged to elaborate and define the introduction of financial education in schools. Within an outcomes-based educational framework stressing the importance of life skills, the Financial Services Board of South Africa managed to introduce financial education in schools' curricula thanks to the support of the Ministry of Education and of the Provincial authorities responsible for the local implementation of national programmes.

The United Kingdom, finally, provides a relevant example of a country where a financial authority has had the autonomy and strong willingness to suggest and back policy directions and that was able to effectively partner with both public institutions and Ministries as a result of support from the government. It also sets out the importance of defining different stages in the creation and implementation of a strategy for financial education in schools: create awareness of the need for financial education and secure the support of the educational system and of teachers in particular.

Australia

The structure of the Australian education system has presented several challenges to the integration of financial education in the school curriculum.

Australia has eight states and territories, each with constitutional responsibility for the delivery of school education and associated curriculum and assessment within their own state-based curriculum framework. Within each state and territory there are also three sectors of education: Government, Catholic, and the Independent school sector. In each jurisdiction schools systems and individual schools have to juggle and respond to local, state and national priorities. These priorities impact on jurisdictional curriculum frameworks and require states and territories to make difficult decisions on how these priorities will be addressed.

Overlaying state education responsibilities are national goals for schooling and national priorities agreed under a Ministerial Council comprised of federal, state and territory education ministers. For the past thirty years the school education curriculum framework in each jurisdiction has had to comply with and support the national goals of schooling and their curriculum has had to align with national statements of learning across English, mathematics, science, civics and citizenship as well as information and communication technology. National funding and testing has been linked to these curriculum areas. Outside of these nationally agreed priority areas, jurisdictions have had flexibility to include other curricula. Until recently, financial education was not seen as a core educational skill across jurisdictions and it was an elective component of secondary schools. A key mechanism in securing political willingness to include financial education in school education was the development of the National Consumer and Financial Literacy Framework. In 2005, the Education Ministers from each state and territory, as members of the then Ministerial Council for Education, Employment, Training and Youth Affairs (MCEETYA)[1], commissioned the development of the Framework. This has ensured ownership of the Framework across all eight jurisdictions.

The Framework was endorsed by all jurisdictions in 2005, and all states and territories agreed that from 2008 it would be integrated into all jurisdictional curricula. Following the negotiation of new national goals for schooling[2] in 2008, the rationale for the Framework was updated in 2009. The advent of the national Australian Curriculum, which is being phased in over 2011–2016[3], prompted a second and more comprehensive review of the Framework in 2011 to ensure the dimensions and progression of student learning were better aligned with the new curriculum. The changes to the Framework were agreed by all education jurisdictions.

Since late 2008, Australia has been undergoing significant reform in the school education sector, including preparing for the phased introduction of a national Australian Curriculum from 2011. The Australian Curriculum, Assessment and Reporting Authority (ACARA), established in 2009, is charged with developing the new Australian Curriculum from Kindergarten to Year 12 in agreed learning areas[4]. State and Territory education departments are responsible for implementing the Australian Curriculum.

The advent of the new national curriculum presented an excellent opportunity to strengthen the consistency and coherence of financial literacy education taught in Australian schools. In 2009-2010, ASIC made one of its key priorities the integration of financial literacy in relevant learning areas of the national curriculum. In partnership with relevant professional associations, and with the support of the Australian Government Financial Literacy Board, ASIC participated actively in the consultation process on the draft curriculum for Mathematics, English and Science. As a result the integration of financial literacy content in these curriculum areas is strengthened. For example, there is a sub-strand in the Mathematics curriculum called 'Money and financial mathematics'. ASIC has continued to advocate strongly for inclusion of financial literacy content and contexts as other curriculum areas are developed. For example, the content of the draft Economics and Business curriculum, due for Ministerial approval in December 2013, includes significant content about consumer and financial literacy.

In 2011, ASIC led a review of the National Consumer and Financial Literacy Framework to better align the dimensions and learning descriptions in the Framework to the structure and content of the new national Australian Curriculum and to take account of both national and international developments in education and financial literacy research and of rapid advances in technology that have impacted greatly on Australians' use of online and digital environments in their everyday lives. The Framework now sets out an agreed national approach to the integration of financial education in the compulsory years of schooling from Foundation to Year 10 and provides guidance on how the subject may be structured to support progressions of learning.

The Australian approach to securing the inclusion of financial literacy in school curricula has been based on using the mechanisms available within well-established educational approaches and cooperative partnerships. The ability to influence public policy and see linkages across government and education has been essential. In developing the original Framework in 2005, consultation was key to inform the national approach. The MCEETYA Working Party who developed the Framework included a highly specialised team of educational experts from all jurisdictions and education sectors who knew the national and jurisdictional educational landscape well, had excellent stakeholder networks and formed productive and respectful relationships. This collaborative approach has continued with the representatives from state and territory education sectors involved in the revision of the Framework in 2011.

Since the National Consumer and Financial Literacy Framework was first agreed in 2005, a significant challenge to the inclusion of financial literacy in the school curriculum has been how to develop teacher capability nationally. In 2007-09 the Australian Government provided funding to develop and fund a national professional learning programme for teachers to raise awareness of the National Consumer and Financial

Literacy Framework and links to state and territory curriculum Frameworks. The government provided further funding to ASIC in the 2011 and 2013 federal budgets to develop and deliver a MoneySmart Teaching professional learning programme and resources to ensure teachers had ready access to the materials they needed to teach financial literacy effectively as part of the Australian Curriculum. All professional learning programs have been delivered either in formal partnership or in collaboration with state and territory education departments.

Brazil

In Brazil, the introduction of financial education in schools was the first priority of the National Strategy (ENEF)[5] established under the leadership of the *Comitê Nacional Educação Financeira* (National Committee for Financial Education, CONEF). It was preceded by the creation of a dedicated institutional structure within the national strategy governing system and by the creation of a co-operation agreement with an association representing the private financial sector. The introduction of financial education took place through a pilot programme in public high schools (see also following section on evaluation).

In November 2007, the Brazilian government formed a working group to develop a National Strategy for Financial Education within the Supervisory and Regulatory Committee of Financial Systems, Capital Markets, Private Insurance and Social Welfare (COREMEC). The working group gathered representatives from the Central Bank of Brazil, the Securities and Exchange Commission of Brazil (CVM), the National Superintendence of Pensions Funds (PREVIC) and the Superintendence of Private Insurance (SUSEP).

COREMEC approved in 2009 a national strategy draft whose different sections were written under the co-ordination of one of the four financial regulators. One of the programmes devised was the introduction of financial education in schools, under the co-ordination of CVM. The other financial regulators made substantial contributions to the review of the action plan and to the guidelines for financial education included in the school curriculum. Notably considerable effort was invested to achieve a high level of involvement and co-operation between the Ministry of Education and other educational authorities from the very start.

Such involvement has been essential given the federal structure of the country. In Brazil, the federal government sets the general standards for schools but does not have direct responsibilities, with a few exceptions, on primary and secondary schools, which are mainly local (municipalities) and regional (states). Both levels have a large degree of autonomy in determining their curriculum.

To deal with this complexity and following the advice of the Ministry of Education, the working group put together a Pedagogical Support Group (*Grupo de Apoio Pedagógico,* GAP) with representatives from the local governments and the 27 states of the Brazilian Federation, the most relevant federal schools, the private sector and the federal government. The group also aimed at providing the technical advice needed to shape the programme in accordance with educational official methodology, as well as to facilitate the inclusion of financial concepts into the normal curriculum of primary and secondary schools.

This body provides pedagogic guidance to all programmes within the national strategy. It was officially established by a federal decree, is hosted by the Ministry of Education and includes members from both educational and financial public institutions:

- The Ministry of Education (MEC), acting as President and serving as Executive Secretariat;

- The Central Bank;

- Securities and Exchange Commission of Brazil (CVM);

- Brazil's National Superintendence for Pension Funds (PREVIC);

- Brazil's Superintendence of Private Insurance (SUSEP);

- National Council of Education (CNE);

- Up to 5 federal educational institutions appointed by MEC;

- National Council of Secretaries of Education (CONSED), the community of education professionals that act in Brazilian State governments, and the National Association of Municipal Education Managers (UNDIME), by invitation.

The creation of this institutional mechanism allowed a permanent dialogue both between financial and education authorities, and between central and local governments.

New Zealand

In 2007, financial literacy was included in the New Zealand Curriculum (NZC)[6]. Developing financial literacy is highlighted as an example of the type of theme that schools could use for effective cross-curricular teaching and learning programmes. It further highlights the fact that all learning should make use of the natural connections that exist between learning areas and that link learning areas to the values and key competencies. The vision of the NZC is that students will be confident, connected, actively involved, lifelong learners. The cross curriculum theme of financial literacy supports this vision by providing a context for students to become:

- enterprising and entrepreneurial contributors to their own well-being and that of New Zealand;

- informed decision makers; and

- financially literate and numerate.

In the New Zealand context, supporting students to become responsible, confident and independent managers of money is ultimately aimed at enabling them to live, learn, work, and contribute as active members of their communities.

The New Zealand's first National Strategy for Financial Literacy (the Strategy) launched in June 2008, has been renewed in 2012 and now includes a five year action plan; implementation of this rests with the many stakeholders involved. The Strategy sets the direction for improving financial literacy in New Zealand. Its focus is on developing the quality of financial education, extending its delivery, sharing what works and working together. The Strategy and action plan are aimed at encouraging agencies and organisations to work together towards a shared understanding of goals and the commitment and pathways to achieve them. The Commission for Financial Literacy and Retirement Income is the secretariat for the Strategy. The Strategy is overseen by a Board of senior government officials, including the Secretary of Education, and is chaired by the chair of a major finance sector body.

In June 2009, the Commission was able to transfer responsibility for the Financial Literacy Framework and for promotion and development of financial education in schools to the Ministry of Education.

This move was also intended to instil a sense of urgency in all schools to fully implement effective financial education programmes. The self-governing structure of the school system in New Zealand does present some opportunities as well as challenges. The school principals as leaders of teaching and learning have a responsibility to plan, with their staff and communities, their school curriculum (aligned with the national curricula - NZC and *Te Marautanga o Aotearoa* -TMoA) and lead what is being taught in their schools.

The New Zealand Qualifications Authority has also made available a set of unit standards for senior secondary schools to provide assessment opportunities in the financial literacy of secondary school students. The use of the unit standards are being monitored for their usage by schools.

The Commission for Financial Literacy and Retirement Income and the Ministry of Education are working closely to develop resources to support teaching and learning in schools. A number of teaching and learning resources, available through the Ministry of Education Website, have been developed with the assistance of a range of providers. Some of the resources aim to link the Personal Financial Management Curriculum, the New Zealand Curriculum and a range of New Zealand Qualifications Authority unit standards.

The Commission also annually facilitates the Money Week held in the first week of September. This is proving to be an excellent way of providing teachers with additional resources and support with a focus on financial capability for a specific week. The Week has featured schools participating in a range of money themed activities including school wide quizzes, competitions, seminars and displays. Moreover, uptake by teachers of the resources is increasing.

South Africa

The Financial Services Board of South Africa (FSBSA) has been a main promoter of financial education in schools in South Africa. The FSBSA is an independent institution established by statute to oversee the South African non-banking financial services industry. The mission of the FSBSA is to promote and maintain a sound financial investment environment in South Africa.

The vision of the consumer education strategy is to see that all South Africans manage their personal and family financial affairs soundly and that irresponsible financial services providers are reported. As part of the Strategy, the FSBSA identified the formal education sector as a key area for creating awareness about financial literacy and consumer education.

The election of the first democratic South African government in 1994 brought about the initiation of processes to restructure the South African educational system to address apartheid inequities. The restructuring brought about the establishment of a national and nine provincial Departments of Education (DoE) to govern the education system in South Africa. In 2009, the DoE was split into the Department of Basic Education (DBE) and the

Department of Higher education and Training (DoHET). The DBE is responsible for formal schooling while the DoHET is responsible for institutes of higher learning. Both departments are responsible for formulating policy, setting norms and standards, and monitoring and evaluating all levels of education within their respective mandates. The DBE shares a concurrent role with the provincial departments of education for school education. The Constitution of South Africa has, however vested substantial power in the provincial legislatures and governments to run educational affairs, subject to a national policy framework. The South African Schools Act, 1996, further devolves responsibility to school level by delegating the governance of public schools to democratically elected school-governing bodies, consisting of parents, educators, non-educator staff and (secondary school) learners.

The role of the DBE is therefore to translate the education policies of government and the provisions of the constitution into a national education policy and legislative framework, which needs to be implemented by the provincial departments. The foundation for these educational changes was based on the development of an outcomes-based curriculum framework which aimed to equip learners with the knowledge, skills and values necessary for self-fulfilment and meaningful participation in society, irrespective of their socio-economic background, culture, race, gender, physical or intellectual ability. It was during the design and development of the National Curriculum Statement (NCS) in 2003, that the FSBSA, together with other stakeholders in the financial sector, made recommendations to the then DoE to enable the inclusion of financial education as part of specific subjects and learning areas. As a result, provision was made for the inclusion of consumer financial education in the learning area Economic and Management Sciences (EMS) for grades R to 9 (5 to 15- year-olds), and in the subjects accounting, mathematics, mathematical literacy, business and economics for grades 10 to 12 (16 to 18- year-olds). In 2010, the NCS was reviewed and was amended to include the Curriculum Assessment and Policy Statements Grades R-12 (CAPS). The phasing-in process of the amended NCS commenced in 2012 and will be completed in 2014. CAPS aimed to simplify the teaching process by making the curriculum more accessible by providing clear topics, teaching plans and assessment strategies.

The amended NCS and the introduction of CAPS resulted in the restructuring of subjects and content knowledge across the curriculum. In terms of CAPS, EMS is to be offered from grades 7-9 (ages 12-15) and will include the 40% of the curriculum being dedicated specifically to the topic of financial literacy. Financial literacy will also be embedded in Accounting, Mathematical Literacy, Consumer Studies and Business Economics for grades 10-12 (ages 16-18). The FSBSA has continued to support the DBE in the promotion of financial literacy through the development of CAPS complaint curriculum material and orientation workshops for teachers. All material developed has been endorsed by the DBE.

In a South African context, convincing the DBE to change policy to include financial education goes hand-in-hand with convincing provincial education authorities to implement programmes approved on a national level. However, the FSBSA managed to gain the support of the Minister of Education for their teacher development programmes. Regular communication with the Minister and/or designated staff including reporting on financial education programmes in the schools has resulted in a valuable relationship between the regulator and the DBE so much so that the FSBSA was and continues to be invited to undertake financial education projects in partnership with the DBE. In 2013, the FSBSA received special commendation from the DBE for their efforts in embedding financial literacy in the school curriculum.

United Kingdom

Initial leadership on financial education issues in the United Kingdom was assumed by the Financial Services Authority (FSA). The FSA was an independent non-governmental body, given statutory powers by the Financial Services and Markets Act 2000 to regulate the financial services industry in the United Kingdom. It was replaced in April 2013 by the Financial Conduct Authority and the Prudential Regulation Authority, with some of its responsibilities given to the Bank of England. Prior to these institutional changes, the FSA responsibilities for financial education were given in 2010 to the Consumer Financial Education Body, now the Money Advice Service (see below).

The Money Advice Service is currently (December 2013) engaging with stakeholders who are involved in financial literacy as part of the development of a revised United Kingdom Strategy for Financial Capability. The strategy will look at financial literacy across the life time of an individual and what is required to support and enable people to take control of their money as best they can and it will be published in spring 2014. Building financial literacy in young people through the development of skills, knowledge and behaviour will be a core focus of the strategy and it will build upon financial literacy and education initiatives that are currently being undertaken.

The initial strong leadership by the FSA has been a significant factor in ensuring that financial education is included in all of the education curricula for each of the four countries in the United Kingdom. One of the four objectives that Parliament set the FSA was to promote public understanding of the financial system, and one of the FSA's strategic aims was to ensure that customers achieved a fair deal.

As part of their work to deliver against these, in autumn 2003, the FSA brought together a partnership of key people and organisations in government, the financial services industry, employers, trades unions, and the educational and voluntary sectors to establish a road map for delivering a step change in the financial literacy of the United Kingdom population. The result of this process was the commitment to lead a National Strategy for Financial Capability, work which began in 2006. One of the seven main programmes in the National Strategy was focused on ensuring that young people in schools develop positive attitudes towards money. This work was informed by the benchmark survey into financial literacy in schools, conducted in 2005. The document, "Creating a Step Change in Schools"[7] was published in light of this research, in 2006, and set out a two-pronged strategy for schools – i) to raise the profile and status of financial literacy in national curricula across the United Kingdom, and ii) to ensure teachers feel confident and competent in delivering personal finance lessons to their pupils.

Complementing and building on the FSA's National Strategy, in 2007 the United Kingdom Government set out its long-term aspirations to improve financial literacy in the United Kingdom including that every child has access to a planned and coherent programme of personal financial education in school. In 2008, the Government and FSA set out a joint action plan for financial literacy which defined how the FSA's National Strategy and a variety of Government programmes would support the shared goal of more financially capable citizens, including a significant joint programme of work to support personal financial education in schools.

In a March 2008 report, the Office for Standards in Education (OFSTED) identified common barriers to the development of personal financial education. Similar barriers have been identified in other studies, such as the Scottish Government's report into financial education in Scottish schools, and National Foundation for Educational

Research's report into the FSA-funded 'Learning Money Matters' programme of the Personal Finance Education Group (pfeg). These included pressure on curriculum time, teachers' lack of subject knowledge and expertise; a lack of awareness of resources and other forms of support and the wide variation in provision in post-16 education.

The FSA's role has been to ensure personal financial education was embedded in education policy frameworks and to ensure that teachers are supported in delivering personal financial education. The FSA's United Kingdom wide remit meant it was well placed to co-ordinate financial literacy provision in schools in England, Scotland, Wales and Northern Ireland. In order to best influence Government policy to include financial literacy within the school curriculum, the FSA worked with education policy experts across the United Kingdom. As education is a devolved function, the FSA worked with policy makers in England, Scotland, Wales and Northern Ireland, identifying where personal finance sits within each policy framework, and showing how personal finance can be embedded in a way that is meaningful to schools. The FSA set up a schools working group in 2004 that was comprised of representatives from key Government departments across the United Kingdom, to ensure buy-in to the approach from the outset of the project. The strategy document "Creating a Step Change in Schools"[8] sets out the outcomes from this working group.

Working with education experts, FSA identified opportunities to input into existing curriculum reform programmes across the United Kingdom, taking the opportunity to raise the profile of financial literacy in national curricula as part of wider curriculum reform. For example, they were able to effectively engage with the secondary school curriculum reform programme in England in 2007. As a result, financial literacy was given a far greater status and profile in secondary schools in England when a new curriculum was implemented in 2008.

Across the United Kingdom, an emphasis on the cross-curricular nature of personal finance education has enabled teachers to integrate aspects of personal finance into existing lessons. Teaching financial literacy through or as part of other subjects helps to give it a place in a crowded curriculum. The FSA has found it was helpful to promote the ways financial literacy can be integrated into existing curricula. For example, many schools taught financial literacy in Personal, Social, Health and Economic (PSHE) education, and in mathematics, but there were opportunities to integrate financial concepts in home economics, English, geography, and drama, for example. By highlighting the cross-curricular nature of financial literacy, the FSA ensured that financial literacy was not seen as another initiative in schools, and that it was something that teachers could integrate within existing curricula.

When engaging with Government, the FSA made appropriate links with high-level government policy. For example, in England one of the five Every Child Matters outcomes is to ensure all children 'achieve economic wellbeing'. FSA promoted the teaching of personal finance in schools to be a key way of contributing to this strategic outcome. Similarly, in Wales the Financial Inclusion Action Plan is closely linked to financial literacy. The FSA has successfully made the case that financial literacy in schools is vital to ensuring the future adult population in Wales understands the financial choices available to them.

The FSA's work and the support, in particular, of key education ministers, has ensured that financial literacy is contained in national curricula across the United Kingdom in varying degrees, typically within personal and social education frameworks and mathematics frameworks. In England, for example, financial literacy is an explicit strand of PSHE education. There are also explicit opportunities to learn about personal finance in mathematics, and citizenship lessons.

From September 2014, finance education (as part of the subject of citizenship) will be compulsory within the National Curriculum in England. Financial education is compulsory for certain age groups in Northern Ireland and Scotland (see Chapter 3, Financial Education Learning Framework in Northern Ireland, United Kingdom; and Financial Education Learning Framework in Scotland, United Kingdom). In Wales, the Literacy and Numeracy Framework (LNF) became a statutory curriculum requirement for schools from September 2013. It is a curriculum planning tool that provides opportunities for developing numeracy skills – including money skills – across the curriculum and lays down the building blocks for financial education from Foundation Phase upwards. It supports all teachers to embed literacy and numeracy in their teaching of the curriculum. It provides learning outcomes/standards, is endorsed by government, and is statutory for ages 5 -14.

However, even with a statutory footing, quality of teaching is not guaranteed and there needs to be adequate teacher training, both as part of initial teacher training and within continuing professional development, to ensure national curricula is taught effectively. Thus it is important for Government to give a clear signal to schools of the importance of personal financial education. This works on three levels: teachers need adequate training and support so they feel confident and competent in delivering personal financial education; schools need to understand the importance of a planned and coherent programme of personal financial education in their school; and financial education needs to have sufficient prominence in Government policy. It is also important for Government, the regulator, the voluntary sector and the financial services industry – the key sectors who work with schools- to understand the contribution each sector makes. The FSA worked strategically with each of these sectors to encourage a co-ordinated, joined up approach to personal finance in schools and to ensure work was complementary and, where possible, not duplicative.

Effective approaches for the introduction of financial education into school curricula

The previous section illustrates the importance of political support and willingness in order to succeed in the development and implementation of financial education programmes in schools. This section focuses on best ways to integrate financial education into school curricula taking into account the specific characteristics of national/regional/local educational systems.

Regular surveys conducted within the OECD/INFE and for the PISA financial literacy assessment from 2008 till 2013 show that a mounting number of countries (over 40 at present) have introduced financial education initiatives in schools (including in elementary and secondary/high schools). Among these, a more limited number of countries have financial education as a compulsory topic or as an integral part of the curriculum (see Table 3.A1.1).

Countries are integrating financial education in various ways. In a minority of countries (in some United States states for example), financial education is a stand-alone subject which is also often optional. In the majority, it is integrated into several subjects through a cross-curricular approach. Mathematics is the most popular subject to include financial education. Other subjects include economics, politics, history, social sciences, home economics, business studies, knowledge about society, enterprise, social and citizen competences, Personal Social Health and Economic Education (PSHE), careers education, work-related learning, learning for life and work, citizenship, language/literature, science, civics, Information and Communications Technology (ICT), moral education, economic and management sciences, accounting and consumer studies.

Whether the integration is cross-curricular or into one subject, the provision of concrete pedagogic tools to teachers for a consistent incorporation in the existing school programme is crucial. In a cross-curricular approach, raising the visibility of financial literacy is very important and the curriculum or the learning framework needs to promote the use of authentic contexts for the delivery of financial literacy. It is also critical for schools to have a curriculum or framework that introduces financial literacy progressively through the different grades. The OECD/INFE survey identified a dozen of countries which have developed full-fledged learning frameworks on financial education adapted to education systems and curricula (see Chapter 3).

This section provides examples of flexible approaches to incorporate financial education into national curricula taken by four countries. Brazil offers the example of a cross-curricular approach developed by Federal and local authorities in the context of a pilot programme in high schools. In the case of New Zealand, financial education is included in the New Zealand Curriculum (NZC) through a cross-curricular approach recommended by the Ministry of Education. In Northern Ireland, financial education is statutory and an integrated-curriculum approach is recommended by the Council for the Curriculum Examinations and Assessment. Finally in South Africa, the Financial Services Board (FSBSA) reached an agreement allowing it to develop classroom resources to be used in a cross-curricular approach. Guidance on how to integrate financial education in schools is also presented in the INFE Guidelines provided in Annex A as well as Chapter 3 on the development of learning frameworks.

Brazil

The Guidelines for Financial Education in Schools (COREMEC, 2009b) approved by the National Committee on Financial Education (CONEF) and drafted in co-operation with stakeholders from federal and local education authorities and national financial institutions part of the Pedagogical Support Group, opted for a cross-curricular approach in the introduction of financial education in schools.

The introduction of financial education in schools is proposed in the context of interrelationship of ideas and phenomena. Schools are called to support the development of values, knowledge and skills that are important for driving an autonomous financial life. The Guidelines identify a group of objectives sought with the implementation of financial education school programmes, relating either to the spatial or the temporal dimension, or the balance of financial life (the equilibrium between consumption and savings ensured by appropriate planning). Throughout the Guidelines, Brazilian authorities stress the linkages between individual actions and their impact on society.

The Guidelines identify spatial and temporal dimensions of financial education. The objectives of the spatial dimension are training for citizenship, teaching to consume and save in an ethical well-informed and responsible manner, offering concepts and tools for autonomous decision-making process based on a change of attitude and training disseminators (by which youth education determines positive spillovers on families and communities). In the temporal dimension, the Guidelines aim at teaching short- mid- and long-term planning, developing the culture of prevention, and providing the possibility of change (social mobility), contents and individual scope.

The pedagogical section of the Guidelines further defines financial education as promoting dialogue between different areas of knowledge, and as such calls for financial education to be introduced as a theme that easily transits among different topics already part of students' curriculum. The Guidelines identify Environment, Work and Consumption, as well as Tax Education as the subjects that would more easily allow for the integration of financial education topics.

The Guidelines apply the spatial and temporal dimensions of financial education also to the development of future materials, for both teachers and students. They underline in particular the need to allow students to face situations that prepare them to manage financial aspects of their future lives addressing their individual situation in the context of other spaces (local, regional, national and global); and to teach students to connect actions of the present to the accomplishment of future goals and dreams.

To meet these criteria, the Guidelines state that pedagogical materials must:

- explore students' lives at the individual and social levels;

- present different learning opportunities that might be used in different areas of learning and subjects;

- suggest activities involving the community;

- consider the importance of the recreational element, depending on age and content;

- provide roadmaps for teachers;

- explore the prior knowledge of students;

- respect cultural diversity and regional differences;

- allow easy customisation to different contexts and updates; and

- indicate the possible use of technological tools and resources as a complement to the teaching.

Finally, in order to adapt to an educational system in which local schools enjoy autonomy from the federal government, Brazilian authorities have devised a flexible implementation approach in which voluntary teachers from different disciplines can opt to teach financial education.

New Zealand

Financial literacy is included in the New Zealand Curriculum (NZC) in New Zealand schools. The NZC encourages teachers and students to look at significant future focused issues such as citizenship and enterprise. Building financial literacy contributes to exploring the issue of citizenship through identifying how values such as community participation influence personal financial goals and actions.

Building financial literacy also encourages links across learning areas, particularly social sciences, mathematics and statistics, as well as English. Financial literacy is readily developed within authentic contexts for learning. It provides students with life skills and also opens pathways for further learning and careers.

The NZC articulates a vision for young people to be "creative, energetic and enterprising; to be confident, connected, actively involved and life-long learners; and will continue to develop the values, knowledge and competencies that will enable them to live full and satisfying lives" and that students are "able to contribute to and participate positively in the community" and "living successful and fulfilling lives" (The New Zealand Curriculum, 2007).

The Ministry of Education's approach has been informed by the earlier work of the Commission for Financial Literacy and Retirement Income. The Commission developed, trialled and independently evaluated an initial financial education framework (see a revised and updated version by the Ministry of Education in Appendix 3.A4). The Commission's work provided evidence about the most effective approaches for financial education that align with the overall focus and approach of the New Zealand Curriculum. These approaches have been further developed by the Ministry of Education.

The Ministry of Education has a dedicated website based on the financial education framework to promote and support teachers to integrate financial literacy into their teaching. The website is part of a wider website developed by the Ministry to support the implementation of the revised NZC.

Cross-curricular approach

Developing financial literacy is promoted as an example of the type of theme that schools could use for effective cross-curricular teaching and learning programmes. It provides an authentic context for linking learning areas such as social sciences, mathematics and statistics, English, business studies, health and technology. Financial literacy also provides a relevant context for strengthening literacy and numeracy skills and understandings, developing the key competencies, and exploring values.

In addition to the popular approaches to teaching financial literacy, the website outlines financial literacy progressions (see Appendix 3.A4) for schools to use as a guide to plan and track student learning. The financial literacy progressions provide specific curriculum-based learning outcomes which fit within the numeracy strand of the curriculum. Building financial literacy is an opportunity to create authentic learning experiences to explore and model the values of fairness, establishing priorities, delayed gratification and family or cultural obligations. When making their own financial decisions, students need to be aware of the impact these may have on other people including family, friends and other community members.

Social-inquiry approach

The financial literacy website provides specific guidance about effective pedagogy when using cross-curricular approaches to developing financial literacy. A social-inquiry approach is recommended that involves students:

- asking questions, gathering information, examining relevant current issues;
- exploring and analysing people's values and perspectives;
- considering the way in which people make decisions;
- reflecting on and evaluating the new understandings they have developed and the responses that may be required.

Creating a supportive environment

Financial literacy lends itself to authentic and engaging contexts for learning. This supports the development of the school curriculum, and meaningful ways for students to connect with their wider lives. It provides opportunities to develop meaningful partnerships with families and communities. Teachers are encouraged to consider how different cultural values affect financial decisions.

Both national curriculums (NZC and TMoA) encourage schools to participate in learning experiences which explore and model values to enable all students to understand and explore New Zealand's rich cultural diversity. These values include concepts such as needs and wants, *manaakitanga* (hospitality) and *whakawhanaungatanga* (family or kin, shared responsibility and collaboration). Forming effective links between school and the cultural contexts in which students grow up is seen as an integral part of creating a supportive learning environment. These 'productive partnerships' ensure that knowledge and expertise is shared between family, community and educators.

School stories

The Ministry of Education's website provides school stories that demonstrate a range of approaches to effective pedagogy described above[9]. These are in the form of written accounts and, in some cases, digital stories. School stories include the following:

- What will a financially literate student look like when they leave Year 8? Using links with local community, workshops were undertaken to answer this question for the school.

- Using the school's inquiry model the Junior School raised money for a class trip. The senior school set a financial goal, and worked towards it for the term.

- A cross-curricular inquiry with students in groups living as a 'family' and managing their money successfully.

- A cross-curricular unit that focused on students understanding the values of excellence and community, being competent at managing themselves while developing skills of budgeting and saving for a day trip away from school.

Northern Ireland

Northern Ireland is among the jurisdictions where financial education is statutory (as of 2010); for all students aged 4-14 years of age. Financial literacy is seen as a key life skill essential to enable young people to develop the knowledge, understanding, skills and confidence to effectively engage in financial decision-making. An integrated-curriculum approach is recommended in which the aims of financial literacy are infused throughout the whole curriculum and all areas of learning are required to explore issues relating to economic awareness.

To support the integration of financial literacy into curricula at primary and secondary level, the Council for the Curriculum Examinations and Assessment (CCEA) has a dedicated financial literacy website[10]. The website provides learning outcomes at five stages: Foundation and Key Stages 1 to 4. Learning outcome statements provide guidance about the most effective approaches to teaching financial literacy.

At the primary level, financial literacy is taught mainly within mathematics but is also addressed, as appropriate, across the curriculum. The following is the statement of learning outcomes and recommended learning activities at the Foundation Stage, provided on the financial literacy website:

> *"During the Foundation Stage, children talk about the need to pay for goods (the exchange of goods for money). They learn about the different ways we can pay (cash, cheque, credit/debit card). They talk about and recognise coins (from 1p to £2) in various contexts and role-play activities, becoming familiar with coins in everyday use. They talk about where money comes from, how we get it and how to keep it safe. Children explore what to spend their money on and how it makes them feel. They talk about what it means to have more than we need and what people can do with extra money"* (Northern Ireland Curriculum website)

At secondary level, financial education is a statutory aspect of learning within mathematics in Key Stage 3, focusing on developing financial knowledge, financial skills and financial responsibility. The statutory statement requires that young people should have opportunities to develop knowledge and understanding of personal finance issues, skills to enable competent and responsible financial decision making, and to apply mathematical skills in everyday financial planning and decision making.

Financial literacy is also a statutory aspect of learning within the home economics learning area, within the key concept of independent living. The statutory statement requires that young people should have opportunities to:

- develop a range of skills to promote independence through planning, managing and using resources;

- explore scenarios for future independent living;

- investigate a range of factors that influence consumer choices and decisions; and

- investigate consumer rights, responsibilities and support available in a range of scenarios.

Within the key element of economic awareness, additional opportunities are provided to highlight financial literacy across all learning areas[11].

At Key Stage 4, financial literacy is covered within the statutory requirements of learning for life and work. Mathematics covers the calculations element of personal finance. Optional courses also include significant opportunities to develop financial literacy such as a new pilot General Certificate of Secondary Education (GCSE) in financial services as well as GCSE courses in economics and home economics.

As well as overall statements of learning outcomes at each stage, the financial literacy website provides specific curriculum links to show how financial literacy is incorporated into various programmes of study. Draft overviews are also provided that show the ways that financial literacy is integrated into the learning areas for which inclusion of financial literacy is statutory at each Stage. The draft overviews provide a list of the specific learning outcomes for each learning area supported by suggested activities[12].

Further guidance about effective practice is provided within the financial literacy website through lesson reviews at each Stage in the form of case studies. The case studies are written by teachers and describe the teaching approaches they used. Most lessons are based on providing students with the opportunity to demonstrate financial literacy in the context of activities involving relevant everyday situations that are of high interest to students.

Examples include: creating a healthy snack on a limited budget; visiting the supermarket to shop for specific items; preparing a budget for a school trip; investigating ways to fund specific consumer purchases. Lessons at Key Stages 3 and 4 also often involve the use of digital media-based resources such as DVDs, websites and interactive online games.

South Africa

In South Africa, the first step to secure the entry of financial education in the formal education sector was the identification of the education sector as a key area for creating awareness about consumer financial education. This entailed researching the possibility of introducing financial education into the National Curriculum Statement (NCS) for specific learning areas and subjects or to have financial education as an extra-curricular activity. The former option prevailed as it was shown that teachers would see anything outside the curriculum as an add-on to their already full programmes.

The FSBSA, together with other stakeholders, made recommendations to the then Department of Education (DoE) to enable the inclusion of financial education as part of specific subjects and learning areas. The next step was to approach the DoE as well as the nine provincial education departments to outline in detail projects and programmes. Although no official memorandum of understanding was signed, an agreement was reached allowing the FSBSA to develop classroom resources in collaboration and in consultation with the DoE and the provinces. This agreement has continued with the Department of Basic Education (DBE) and the FSBSA has provided various Curriculum Assessment and Policy Statements compliant resources to support teachers, especially, in the areas of Economic Management Sciences (EMS), Accounting and Mathematical Literacy.

Tools to support the introduction of financial education in schools

Training the teachers

The importance of training teachers is underlined by most countries as a key component of a successful introduction of financial education in schools. Indeed one of the factors that will influence the educational system in its support for financial education is the availability of high quality teaching material together with training and other support for teachers. Furthermore, while support for financial education in schools may be secured at the governmental level, this will have little impact on student learning unless teachers are actively encouraged and supported to incorporate financial education into their teaching programmes.

Such training can be provided as part of an initial teachers course, or later in their professional life as part of lifelong training. In both cases, it should be provided by qualified staff and following predefined approved guidelines. Trainers should in particular be aware of the requirements of the educational curriculum and be familiar with the pedagogic tools that will later be used by teachers in their classes.

In addition, the majority of countries that have financial education in schools have also developed a wide variety of pedagogical resources available to support teachers in the classroom: printed material, interactive tools through the Internet, student competitions, games and films. These are elaborated by the Ministries of Education but also by national banks, the private sector and NGOs.

The following five case studies describe the training provided to support financial education in Australia, Canada and the Province of British Columbia, England, Japan, and South Africa.

Each case study provides a useful example for policy makers. Australia illustrates the need to put financial education into perspective, stressing the synergies with the entire school curriculum; Canada shows the importance of an appropriate choice of delivery method, through a wide use of webcasts and web conferences; England offers an interesting perspective on the involvement of a charity and its collaboration with the private sector; Japan provides interesting insight on the development of an effective national network for training and research using the local branches of the Central Bank; and finally South Africa is an example of the integration within the educational system through a point-based system for the professional development of teachers.

Australia

In 2005, the Australian Government established the Financial Literacy Foundation within the Department of Treasury to raise awareness of consumer issues and encourage all Australians to better manage their money. From July 2008, the responsibility for financial literacy policy and the functions of the Financial Literacy Foundation moved to the Australian Securities and Investments Commission (ASIC).

In 2007-09, the Australian Government funded the development and implementation of a national professional learning programme for teachers. The professional learning package comprised a facilitator guide (notes and multimedia supports), a teacher guide and a DVD designed to raise awareness among teachers about the National Consumer and Financial Literacy Framework and assist them to build their understanding of the context for consumer and financial literacy in schools with particular emphasis on integration within the existing state and territory curricula.

A website for educators was established at that time. This website was re-developed by ASIC in 2011-12 to become the MoneySmart Teaching website - a hub of free financial literacy resources and professional learning materials for educators (www.teaching.moneysmart.gov.au). Resources on the MoneySmart Teaching website include digital activities and videos for use in the classroom, developed by ASIC and a range of providers such as other government departments, consumer protection agencies, banks and other financial institutions. Teachers can search for resources by year level, learning area, audience and resource type.

The website also houses the MoneySmart Teaching materials developed by ASIC:

- MoneySmart Teaching professional learning packages for primary and secondary schools. These packages include a Facilitator Guide, professional learning workshops to embed financial literacy teaching across a learning area, a faculty and the whole school, a Teacher Guide, and units of work mapped to the Framework and Australian Curriculum.

- Information about how to become a MoneySmart School.

- A suite of interactive digital resources (for computers, iPads and interactive whiteboards) which complement the units of work and can also be used as stand-alone resources.

- High-value videos for use in the classroom and for professional learning.

- A personal financial learning programme (video, newsletter, podcasts).

- Two interactive online professional learning modules for teachers.

Over 8 000 teachers across Australia have been trained so far using the MoneySmart Teaching Primary and Secondary professional learning packages across over 90 schools who were involved in trialling the units of work developed to support teachers. ASIC aims to reach 24 000 teachers over the next few years.

Canada and the Province of British Columbia

The Financial Consumer Agency of Canada (FCAC) was established in 2001 as an independent federal government body to protect and inform consumers of financial services. The Minister of Finance's 2007 budget speech recognised financial literacy for young people and adults as a priority. In that budget, the Government of Canada allocated funding over two years to financial literacy, mandating FCAC to strengthen financial skills among youth. In its 2008 budget, the Government of Canada provided additional ongoing funding to FCAC to support efforts to improve financial literacy in Canada.

As a federal regulator, FCAC has no formal role in public schooling. It can undertake public information and education campaigns, but these are of limited reach outside of public school systems. The challenge, therefore, was to extend financial education initiatives that would be effective and engaging for schools, teachers and students, without encroaching on provincial and territorial education jurisdiction.

The surveys undertaken by FCAC showed that many teachers are uncomfortable teaching financial life skills because they are not confident in their own financial literacy. Drawing on the advice of the British Columbia Securities Commission (BCSC) partners, FCAC addressed this challenge in the following two ways.

First, through the provision of material that is comprehensive and contains all the information teachers need to conduct the activities. Links and notes provide additional information for teachers who wish to access it. A teacher training plan was developed to deliver training through workshops or electronically via webcasts and web conferencing using a train-the-trainer model. Second, through training specialists that deliver the training through web conferences and on-line self-directed training and the teacher champions deliver workshops in person at teacher conferences, professional development sessions and in school workshops that they coordinate.

England, United Kingdom

The organisation most closely involved with the delivery of financial education resources and support to schools in England is the Personal Financial Education Group (pfeg). Pfeg is an independent charity helping schools to plan and teach personal finance relevant to students' lives and needs. Pfeg was founded in 2000 and receives funding from a variety of supporters in Government, the statutory sector and the financial services industry. In 2010, there were five regional **pfeg** offices established in London and the South East, the North West, the North East, South West and Central England with more than 20 full-time expert consultants and 26 freelancers working with schools to plan and deliver financial education.

From June 2008 until March 2011, pfeg ran the My Money programme, developed and delivered for all schools in England on behalf of the Department for Children, Schools and Families (DCSF, now replaced by the Department of Education, DfE). It was the first project to provide an integrated approach to personal finance education from when a child first starts school through to the end of secondary school. Within the framework of this project, the programme provided local authorities with support and training to help them to get personal finance into every school in their care and would also give schools access to high quality teaching resources and information across the primary and secondary sectors to help children and young people learn what they need to know to manage their money well.

There is so far no dedicated government funding for teacher training or continuing professional development relating to financial education in England. The charity pfeg however works in consultation with the Department for Education (DfE) to provide initial teacher training, continuing professional development, resources and support to teachers through a number of programmes with the support of several financial services organisations and grant funders. In addition, the education regulatory body Ofsted is currently putting together a guide for teachers on PSHE to provide teachers with a range of examples to inform teaching. The pfeg website provides case studies showing how teachers in different types of school and learning contexts can integrate financial literacy into their own school curriculum. The case studies explore both timetabled curriculum lessons and various 'off timetable' enrichment days (for example, enterprise day).

Pfeg's Volunteer Network brings together volunteers with expertise in the financial services industry with teachers in the classroom. Since its inception in 2006, teachers and students have found it valuable to be able to draw on the volunteers' specialist knowledge and experience.

Japan

The Central Council for Financial Services Information (CCFSI) has taken the leading role in promoting and supporting financial education in Japanese schools. The Central Council is an organisation consisting of the representatives of financial and economic organisations, the media, consumer groups, etc., experts, and the deputy governor of the Bank of Japan, with the director-generals of related authorities, including the FSA, and the executive director of the Bank of Japan taking part as advisers. The CCFSI Secretariat is hosted by the Public Relations Department, Bank of Japan.

In 2007, CCFSI published the "Financial Education Programme" with the subtitle of "How to Cultivate the Ability to Live in Society". The programme was developed with the involvement of scholars, officials from the Ministry of Education, Culture, Sports, Science and Technology (Ministry of Education) and others who have influence over the revision of the National Curriculum. The programme provides an overview of financial education goals and learning outcomes for primary, secondary and high school students; describes the most effective ways to introduce financial education in schools and provides model teaching plans for every major subject in primary, secondary, and high schools, written by experienced teachers.

The new National Curriculum, published by the Ministry of Education in March 2008 and 2009, includes contents of financial education in a number of statutory subjects such as social studies, home economics, and moral education in primary, secondary, and high school. The Guidelines associated to the new National Curriculum were implemented in elementary, junior and high-schools in 2011, 2012 and 2013 respectively. Because of the increased importance placed on financial education, CCFSI has recognised the increasing need to provide training and materials to support teachers to teach financial literacy.

CCFSI has a long history of involvement and achievements in training, support, and provision of educational resources. More recently, Local Councils for Financial Services Information, the Bank of Japan, Government, local governments, governmental organisations, associations of financial institutions, consumer organisations and non-profit organisations have also started to promote financial education and are providing educational materials, books on good practices and holding seminars to disseminate good practice. CCFSI is working to promote the exchange of information on the publication of educational materials and other activities concerning financial education.

CCFSI organised the National Conference on Pecuniary Education from 1973 until 2003. The purpose of the conference was to exchange effective methods of pecuniary education. Teachers of designated research schools on pecuniary education and supervisors of school education attended the Conference.

The Local Councils for Financial Services Information have also organised local conferences for promoting exchange of practical achievements between designated research schools on pecuniary and financial education. Local councils for financial services information located in each prefecture provide neutral and impartial information and support for study of the economy and finance. Each of the 47 councils consists of the association of financial and economic organisations, financial institutions, a superintendent of schools, the association of broadcasting companies, and the officials of local government in the prefecture. Chairpersons of the Local Councils are either the governor of the prefecture or the head of the branch of the Bank of Japan. The Local Councils are funded by their members and the CCFSI. The secretariat offices of the Local Councils are located in the local government or in the branch of the Bank of Japan.

Since 2002, CCFSI and Local Councils for Financial Services Information have organised seminars of financial education to support teachers to introduce financial education, with over 150 seminars a year now being held. Officials from the Ministry of Education and the local educational committees are invited to give speeches at the seminars to deepen teachers' understanding on the need of financial education in schools. CCFSI and the Local Councils have asked educational committees to include the contents of financial education in the seminars which they plan as statutory training courses for teachers.

Moreover, financial services information advisers designated by CCFSI and volunteers from other institutions are also invited by schools to give financial education lectures.

South Africa

All resources and materials developed for teachers are mediated to the teachers through specifically designed workshops. As teacher training is the prerogative of the Department of Education (DBE), the workshops serve to assist teachers in using the resource effectively in the classroom through demonstration lessons. It further serves to create awareness among teachers on personal financial planning issues.

In terms of the South African Council of Educators (SACE) Act of 2000, no person is permitted to practise as an educator unless he/she is registered with the Council. SACE has thus developed a Professional Development (PD) point allocation system. All financial education courses administered through the FSBSA will be registered on the system once SACE's system is ready. To date, one programme, the mathematical literacy programme "Managing your Money", has been registered. This will provide teachers with official recognition for financial education courses.

Resources and pedagogic materials

As mentioned in the INFE Guidelines (see Annex A), together with training, the access of teachers to quality and effective resources is critical in order to teach financial education in schools with confidence.

The availability and easy access to objective and effective quality tools is essential at an early stage and should subsequently be promoted and monitored in order to ensure teachers are provided with the best resources on financial education. In some countries, such resources might already be available: the institution in charge of financial education should thus focus on mapping the existing material and choose the most appropriate. In other countries, such resources might not exist, and it may be necessary to develop them from scratch, for example through the creation of ad hoc working groups, or through learning from other countries.

Amongst the countries featured in the case studies several criteria were used for the identification and the development of suitable resources on financial education. In some countries, materials were made available without any co-ordination between concerned institutions, while others had some form of co-ordination, for example, with school books being certified by the Ministries of Education.

Each selected case study below exemplifies relevant practices in developing and making accessible financial education tools and materials.

The Canadian case highlights the need to carefully review all existing pedagogic resources before partnering with an institution in order to improve the quality of materials and make them suitable for a national audience; England shows how a teaching programme can be successfully adapted in a co-ordinated fashion to suit different ages and to incorporate specific programmes on an *ad hoc* basis; Japan illustrates the importance of co-opting experienced teachers in the design of new educational material and the value of interactive activities performed in real-life scenarios; South Africa is a good example of the need to adapt resources to specific learning outcomes in line with the requirements of the national curriculum; finally the United States highlights that the presence of a clearinghouse on existing tools for financial education in schools can prove particularly relevant especially in the context of a very diversified federal educational system.

Canada and the Province of British Columbia

The Financial Consumer Agency of Canada (FCAC) first reviewed existing initiatives and programmes in Canada in order to seek out the best programmes available and to avoid duplication. They planned to adapt the most successful ones for national use, where appropriate, and make them accessible in both official languages (English and French). The review led FCAC to a unique teaching resource developed by the British Columbia Securities Commission (BCSC) called Planning 10, a programme that was being used successfully to teach a mandatory course on personal finances to Grade 10 students in British Columbia (BC). The FCAC partnered with the BCSC to build upon this initiative and extend it across Canada. The outcome is a multi-level education resource called "The City, A Financial Life Skills Resource", launched in September 2008 and available in both English and French.[13]

"The City" consists of a free 11-part teacher-led web resource for youth aged 15 to 18 in schools and a self-directed online component. It aims to engage youth by using a web-based hands-on approach to learning. It makes financial concepts easy to understand and provides practice in real-life skills. Students use realistic financial documents to practice financial activities relating to topics such as budgeting, saving, credit and debt, insurance, taxes and investing. By the end of the course, they prepare a financial plan for the years after they leave school. The resource features two components: a classroom resource for teachers comprised of 11 learning modules and 10 interactive, self-directed online modules for teachers, youth and members of the general public. The online modules parallel the in-class modules, but adapt the activities for the online learning environment. All resources are designed to be self-contained and easy to use, whether individually, in an informal community setting or in a classroom.

Since FCAC has no formal role in the public school system, a variety of strategies have been adopted to promote acceptance of The City among educators. They created a cross-Canada teacher review committee to ensure that teachers would be comfortable with the teaching approach; that the content and level would be appropriate to learners aged from 15 to 18; and that the resource would meet prescribed learning outcomes for each province and territory. The FCAC worked with partners, such as the provincial securities commissions and the Canadian Bankers Association, to ensure that the activities accurately reflect current financial issues. Teachers can download complete in-class resources (including curriculum connections for their province or territory) or order a printed binder at cost.

Drawing on the experience of the BCSC in British Columbia, FCAC enrolled teacher champions in each province and territory – that is, teachers on contract to FCAC who work to increase awareness of The City and to promote its acceptance among teachers and education authorities. Teacher champions have approached their education authorities (except in the Province of Quebec) to discuss listing the resource as an approved teaching resource for the appropriate courses. As of September 2009, the resource was listed as an approved resource in five of thirteen jurisdictions, with an additional three jurisdictions piloting courses where The City is a component within the proposed new curriculum. For example, in New Brunswick, The City comprises one-third of a new course called Business Organisation Management that is being piloted in the 2009-10 school year. In Prince Edward Island, The City became part of the new Grade 10 Career Explorations and Opportunities course that was being piloted in selected English and French schools in 2009.

FCAC also works with the industry to promote The City. The Canadian Bankers Association promotes "The City" through its in-school initiative, "Your Money", in which members of the association visit classrooms across the country to talk with students about financial issues. As of 31 March 2009, two hundred and fifty-eight seminars were held and a total of 7.451 students participated in these seminars.

The resource has been recommended by Curriculum Services Canada, a pan-Canadian standards agency for quality assurance in learning products and programmes, to support curriculum in the areas of personal development, career planning, mathematics, business, economics, family studies, consumer studies, enterprise and entrepreneurship studies and alternative education. It was also recommended by *Le Centre Canadien de Leadership en Évaluation* (Canadian Centre for Leadership in Evaluation, CLÉ) as a financial education resource to support courses taught in French language secondary schools throughout Canada.

England, United Kingdom

My Money Week is a personal finance education initiative organised in 2013 for its 5th consecutive year. The high profile annual money awareness week highlights the need for parents and the wider community to gain skills and confidence in financial matters to support young people's learning in school. The first My Money Week took place in June 2009. It reached since its inception over 2.5 million students, and aims at improving financial literacy for students in primary and secondary schools. The Week is designed to be a flexible programme, within which schools can undertake a variety of activities using diverse curriculum subjects. pfeg provides pedagogical resources, experts' consultancy, and activity packs.

At the secondary level, pfeg's "Learning Money Matters" programme, funded by the FSA first and by the Money Advice Service (MAS), ran from 2006 to 2011 and offered free advice, support and resources to schools and teachers who wanted to teach personal finance education in a way that would fit an individual school's needs, with the help of a nationwide network of consultants. These consultants offered a range of free support to teachers to enable them to become confident and competent in delivering financial education to their pupils.

Additional support at the secondary level in England has been provided by the financial education framework "Guidance on Financial Capability in the Curriculum: Key Stage 3 and 4". Developed by the Department for Children, Schools and Families (DCSF) in 2008, the framework was designed to help school staff and others working with secondary schools to understand financial literacy and to plan and implement personal financial education as part of the new secondary curriculum.

At the primary level, pfeg has developed "What Money Means", a five-year programme that ran from 2007 to 2012 to increase the quantity and quality of personal financial education. It was designed to give younger children a foundation for managing their money now and in the future. The programme aimed to help teachers feel confident in tackling money with children of primary age. It offered resources and support to help teachers plan and teach personal finance in ways that fit into existing activities and curriculum plans, and at no cost to them. The programme was made available to all primary schools in England in 2011.

Pfeg also acts as a 'one-stop-shop' for teachers to find resources to support financial education. These are made available on a searchable database on the pfeg website14. The pfeg Quality Mark accreditation system ensures that resources and materials for teaching financial literacy are suitable, effective and of the highest educational quality, covering Year 1 to Year 13. To date, more than 50 resources have been awarded the Quality Mark. All pfeg Quality Mark resource providers are required to adhere to a rigorous code of practice. The Quality Mark is awarded to resources that are accurate and up-to-date; match curriculum requirements; are easily available, adaptable and low cost; cover an appropriate range of financial topics and have been developed in partnership with teachers and tested in schools.

Japan

The Central Council for Financial Services Information (CCFSI) publishes financial educational materials and videos and provides information on their website to support financial education. CCFSI involves experienced teachers in developing educational materials and organises editorial committees with excellent teachers and principals as well as scholars and lawyers. The materials reflect the opinions and best practices provided by the teachers. Effective teaching practices have been selected from hundreds of practices reported from designated research schools on financial education. They are also selected from research papers written by experienced teachers and submitted to the public education centres. Effective practices for financial education are provided for most subjects including social studies, home economics, homeroom activities, integrated studies, moral education, mathematics, Japanese language and the arts.

Various activities have been found to be effective in fostering students' interest and deepening their understanding, including role-playing, introducing real-life-scenario activities such as auctions or exchanges, cultivation and sales of vegetables, setting up and running a company.

The following guides have been produced for teachers: Beginners Guide to Financial Education, Financial Education Programme and the Financial Education Guidebook. These guides provide examples of effective practice in financial education and include worksheets developed by teachers that users can easily copy or download to use with their own students.

The following are the most popular student resources, some of which have been produced with accompanying teacher guides:

- "Are You Really Rich?": A resource mainly for high school and college students and adults. It provides basic knowledge on various types of credit cards, contracts, interest rates, and guarantees. It also nurtures sound attitudes toward money which helps averting multiple debt problems. It provides advice on how to solve such problems. The teacher's guide describes the aims of the resource and practical ways to use the educational material. It also explains terminology, related laws, and social background related to multiple debt problems.

- "You are Self-Reliant Now": Workbook developed to provide students with basic economic knowledge necessary to live self-reliantly. Teacher's guide provides the same kind of information as explained above.

- Pocket Money Account Book: A small notebook for recording personal money. This is also provided for primary school pupils as an educational material at their teachers' request.

- "What would you do if you got 1 000 000 yen?": a cartoon booklet for pupils of primary and secondary schools. It explains the role of money and gives knowledge on contracts and various types of credit cards using cartoons so that pupils can enjoy studying.

- Educational videos: for kindergarten, primary, secondary, and high school students and for adults.

Materials are sent to schools free of charge upon request by teachers and about seven hundred thousand copies have been published and distributed of the most popular materials.

South Africa

A major priority for the Department of Basic Education (DBE) is to provide teachers with cost effective, readily usable resources for use in the classroom. Accordingly, the FSBSA developed resources for teachers with actual lesson plans for identified learning areas and subjects. The resources were designed in line with the requirements of the National Curriculum and were updated to be CAPS compliant. The resources targeted specific learning areas and subjects as well as specific grades and included lesson plans and possible assessments.

The following materials were developed:

Managing your Money: a Mathematical Literacy Resource for Teachers – Grades 10, 11 and 12.

The FSBSA, in partnership with the South African Insurance Association (SAIA), contracted a service provider to develop a Mathematical Literacy Resource, "Managing your Money", for teachers of Grades 10, 11 and 12. The initial resource was a 36 page booklet for each of the grades and contained ten lessons on financial literacy that were compliant with the NCS for Mathematical Literacy. A total of 20 600 "Managing Your Money" resource files were printed and distributed at 123 workshops to 7 720 teachers between 2008 and 2010. In 2012, the resource was updated to be CAPS compliant. This entailed a rewrite to ensure content was still relevant. The updated resource included three 64-page booklets, one targeted at each of the three grades and included two posters, one depicting "money management rules" (grade 10) and "Who do I complain to?" (Grade 11). Sixty copies of updated resource were printed and distributed to the nine Provincial Departments of Education. In 2013 the resource and workshops were endorsed by the South African Council for Educators (SACE) and 15 Continual Professional Development (CPD) points will be awarded for teachers who attended the "Managing your Money" workshops.

Money in Action: a guide to personal financial management – Grades R to 12

The FSBSA in partnership with the Financial Service Consumer Education Foundation and the SAIA contracted e-Learning Laboratory (e-Lab) to develop the digital resource "Money in Action" for teachers and learners. The resource was endorsed by the Department of Basic Education (DoE) and was well received by teachers. With the introduction of the Curriculum Assessment and Policy Statements (CAPS) in 2013 the resource needed to be updated.

This rewrite was undertaken in conjunction with the DBE. The resource included a 71 page booklet consisting of ten activities across the three grades. The resource was also supplemented by a poster focussing on entrepreneurship with a supporting lesson. The booklet was presented in workshops with officials from the Provincial Departments of Education and district officials. Nine workshops, reaching 360 education officials were conducted nationwide, as part of the DBE CAPS orientation programme. The aim of the workshop was to assist officials on how to orientate teachers on the use of the resource. A total of 52.100 copies were printed and distributed to teachers nationwide.

A Financial Guide for Youth

The FSBSA, with the assistance of a professor at the University of South Africa, developed content for a Financial Guide for Youth. The FSBSA then contracted a service provider to design, lay out and print the booklet. Another service provider was contracted to conduct workshops in the nine provinces. In total 15 700 booklets were printed and 108 workshops were held with 3 010 attendees (Grade 12 school learners, school leavers, university students and first time workers/salary earners) from January to April 2009. The main topics in the booklet include: financial planning, banks and what they do, studying, working for yourself, working for someone else, and what do you do if you feel you've been cheated (recourse). The guide has proven a vital resource in all education programmes. Currently the FSBSA is undertaking a review of the Financial Guide for Youth to ensure it remains relevant and appealing to the target market. The review includes narrowing the age focus to 16-23 (from 16-35), reviewing the content to reflect recent developments in the financial sector, reviewing the design and layout and making the language more 'youth appealing'.

United States

Convened in 1995, the Jump$tart Coalition is a not-for-profit organisation that consists of 180 businesses, financial and educational organisations and 47 affiliated state coalitions providing advocacy, research, standards and educational resources to improve the financial literacy of youth.

A key national-level resource provided by the Coalition is the 'National Standards in K-12 Personal Finance Education'[15], first developed in 1998. The standards are intended to provide a personal financial education design and evaluation framework for school administrators, teachers, curriculum specialists, instructional developers and educational policy makers.

As such, the National Standards represent the framework of an ideal personal finance curriculum, portions of which may not be appropriate for individual instructors and students. The Coalition leaves it up to various stakeholders to decide how to address the topics in the National Standards. Educators can use the standards and expectations to design new personal finance units or courses, or to integrate concepts into existing courses. (Jump$tart Coalition for Personal Financial Literacy, 2007)

To help educators to make effective use of the standards and to support effective teaching practice for financial education, the Coalition provides additional resources. These are a personal finance clearinghouse of teaching resources, national best practices guidelines and teacher workshops.

The Clearinghouse

One of Jump$tart's aims is to identify high-quality personal finance materials for educational use. The Clearinghouse is a database of personal finance resources available from a variety of education providers such as Government, business and non-profit organisations. The Clearinghouse enables teachers to identify appropriate educational materials by grade level, format and content category.

The Clearinghouse uses the Educational Materials Review Checklist as a guide in the selection of materials to be included in the database. Materials are reviewed for accuracy, completeness and appropriateness for educational use but inclusion in the database does not constitute endorsement of the materials.

National Best Practices Guidelines

The Coalition provides recommended best practices to support the development of financial education resources and their selection. The guidelines cover the following criteria: objectivity; alignment to standards; teaching and learning; target group; accuracy and up-to date; availability and accessibility; evaluation and assessment.

Ways to ensure the sustainability and efficiency of programmes

Role of private financing: importance and challenges

Appropriate, commensurate and long-term resources are essential to the development of financial education in schools. The amount and nature of resources determines the scope of financial education programmes, their effectiveness and their duration. Against a background in which public funds for schools are often more easily channelled towards the standard components of school curricula, the involvement of the private sector can provide the input needed for the sustainability of the development of a learning framework for financial education in schools. Private funding can also bring additional benefits, such as the technical expertise on financial services of private stakeholders, which can complement the pedagogical expertise of the educational sector.

However, the involvement of the private sector can also give rise to the risk of conflicts of interest. Consequently, countries that took advantage of the availability of private funding have also developed means to monitor and manage possible conflicts of interest with the commercial activities of the institutions involved[16]. These experiences underline the importance of keeping the monitoring of the use of private funds in the hands of the public sector, an independent regulatory body or a recognised not-for-profit organisation (see also Box A1.2 in Annex A).

In some countries the private sector funds a variety of resources and projects through the provision of in-kind and financial resources (among these Malaysia, the United Kingdom and the Czech Republic). The role of such private entities varies. Their role may include inputs for learning frameworks, organisation of workshops to train teachers or students, development of materials and lesson plans, distribution of materials and promoting awareness.

Other cases illustrate the existence and importance of public-private partnerships: in Australia, through the Australian regulator's financial literacy education strategy; in Canada with partnerships between the Financial Consumer Agency of Canada, the Canadian Bankers Association; in Japan through the Central Council for Financial Services Information (CCFSI) and Local Committees for Financial Services Information in partnership with the private sector; and finally in South Africa with the creation of an independent trust that serves as a vehicle for donors' support, the Financial Services Consumer Education Foundation.

In countries where the private sector is actively involved, and as highlighted by the INFE Guidelines, strong attention has been paid to potential conflicts of interest arising in particular from the creation and provision of pedagogic material. For most, assurance was provided through government leadership or independent committees of experts drafting guidelines, checking that materials correspond to the curricula and assessing them for hidden adverts. The Czech Republic, the United Kingdom and the United States have created standards specifying that financial education should develop and increase financial literacy but not serve as a marketing tool for products and services.

In addition, the involvement of the private sector reinforces the need for a certification or accreditation process for related resources: this applies both to the provision of material (to avoid the presence of branding and marketing messages), to the development and organisation of training, and to the active involvement in classroom teaching by volunteers.

The Financial Stability Board of South Africa developed a new and neutral logo for material developed through partnerships. Such requirement is clearly stated on the partnership's contract, which also clarifies that industry marketing may only appear on a false cover attached to the approved materials. The United Kingdom has the pfeg 'Quality Mark' as a method of quality assurance so teachers know that the materials are accurate and match curriculum requirements.

The following case studies provide examples of different approaches to the funding of financial education programmes. In Brazil, the private sector, through a dedicated association devoted to financial education, is responsible for raising funds for school programmes (in addition to public funding). In Malaysia, there is extensive private sector involvement in funding financial education in schools, with Bank Negara Malaysia taking a strong leadership role in collaboration with the Ministry of Education. In contrast, in the United Kingdom, the Government and the private sector share responsibility for the funding of financial education in schools. Private sector funding occurs either directly to specific programmes or indirectly via the mechanism of the levy on the financial services sector.

In all three countries, the private sector provides significant in-kind support through the provision of volunteers who provide expert advice to schools and processes are in place to ensure possible conflicts of interest are avoided.

Concerning the risk of possible conflicts of interest, the cases selected are a good illustration of different ways of managing such risk: Brazil incorporates the private sector in the structure of the national strategy, to retain monitoring and oversight over programmes implementation. Malaysia opts for a centralised approach in which the Ministry of Education monitors the activities of financial institutions, in the United Kingdom it is the responsibility of individual schools and teachers to decide over the suitability of a resource but with the assistance of professional support programmes and thanks to the strong role played by a quality certificate awarded by the pfeg to private sector resources and by a forthcoming Code of Practice being developed by the Money Advice Service.

Brazil

The implementation of the financial education programme takes place through a public-private partnership between the Financial Education Committee (CONEF) and the Association of Financial Education of Brazil (AEF–Brazil). This Association, which obtained the legal status of "organisation of public interest" (*Organização da Sociedade Civil de Interesse Público*, OSCIP), is a not-for-profit entity founded by the Brazilian Financial and Capital Markets Association (ANBIMA), the Brazilian Federation of Banks (FEBRABAN), the Brazilian Insurance Confederation (CNSEG), and Brazil's major stock exchange, BM&FBOVESPA. The AEF serves two purposes: it provides a balanced representation of the private sector within the national strategy and allows raising funds from additional private sources, without being a direct expression of specific corporate interests.

Conflict of interests are avoided by the structure of the AEF itself, where corporate interests of single financial entities are diluted through the mediation of industry associations, and by the partnership agreement in place between the financial education committee (CONEF) and the AEF.

The Partnership Agreement between CONEF and the AEF is currently valid for 5 years and renewable. Under this Agreement, CONEF defines and presents the national strategy's general guidelines annually to the AEF. The AEF is then responsible for the definition of an implementation action plan that it must submit to CONEF for approval. During the implementation phase, the AEF acts as a repository of the information received from schools, allowing CONEF to monitor reports with the results obtained and to establish a general diagnostic of the situation on the ground.

Malaysia

Public-private partnerships have been a key feature of the promotion and provision of financial education in Malaysian schools since the late 90s. There is currently a proposal to introduce financial education in schools into core subjects as of 2014 in primary schools and as of 2017 in secondary schools. Until now, most financial education has occurred through co-curricular rather than curriculum integrated activities and financial institutions have provided significant funding as well as in-kind support for these initiatives. The involvement of financial institutions in the financial education programme is part of their corporate and social responsibility and financial institutions are encouraged to play a significant role in financial education.

Specific public-private partnerships have been developed through collaboration between Bank Negara Malaysia, the Ministry of Education (MoE) and financial institutions since the launch of the Schools Adoption Programme (SAP) in 1997. Under the SAP, 10 000 Government-funded schools have been adopted by the financial institutions, including schools for children with disabilities. The financial institutions conduct activities relating to banking, insurance and basic financial knowledge and provide an opportunity for school children to have a bank account. It is worth noting that under existing proposals to introduce financial education in core subjects, the SAP platform would continue to play an important role in reinforcing delivery of the subjects in the classroom and in supporting teacher through technical advice (both workshops and guidance).

Bank Negara Malaysia is responsible for coordinating the SAP and for promoting financial education in schools. The Bank allocates an annual budget for the implementation of teacher workshops, development and production of educational materials, maintenance and enhancement of the financial education website[17], promotional activities and prizes for financial education competitions. The Bank has made a long-term commitment to elevating the financial literacy of school children. Other financial institutions also allocate funds to organise activities related to financial education in their adopted schools and to produce financial education materials.

The SAP has been complemented by several other initiatives. These are:

- Student Financial Club (SFC) - a SFC has been established in more than 2000 schools under the SAP since 1999. As part of their co-curricular activities, students who join the clubs engage in money and finance related activities through workshops, visits to financial institutions, knowledge sharing and games.

- Pocket Money Book: introduced in 1998 to educate and assist students to manage their pocket money and to take control of their personal finance. More than 7.9 million books have been distributed.

- Financial education website: In 2004, Bank Negara Malaysia, in collaboration with the Ministry of Education created and launched a financial education website as an interactive financial education tool.

The Bank has worked closely with the MoE. For example, in 2005 a guidebook for teachers-in-charge of SFC was prepared by Bank Negara Malaysia in collaboration with the MoE. To further assist teachers in conducting financial education activities, lesson plans with outlined modules and activities on financial education were distributed to all schools in 2008[18]. The lesson plans were developed at teacher workshops with the contribution of adoptive financial institutions and were compiled by Bank Negara Malaysia.

Bank Negara' Malaysia's efforts are complemented by the contribution of partners such as the Securities Industry Development Corporation, the National Co-operative Organisation of Malaysia, Malaysian Association for the Blind and the relevant government ministries and agencies.

The table below summarises the contributions made by the key stakeholders.

Organisation	Roles
Bank Negara Malaysia in collaboration with the MoE and adoptive financial institutions under SAP	<ul><li>Structure the financial education programme framework for school children</li><li>Organise workshops to train teachers in conducting financial education activities as part of their professional development</li><li>Organise financial education workshops for school children</li><li>Develop materials such as guidebooks and lesson plans to facilitate teachers in conducting activities relating to financial education</li><li>Develop and distribute effective financial education materials such as Pocket Money Book (including Braille version), financial education website, leaflets and brochures</li><li>Promote awareness of the financial education programmes for children</li><li>Organise "Financial Awareness Week" at a different state each year to enhance engagement with the community at large, including school children in the locality</li></ul>
Private sector such as Securities Industry Development Corporation	<ul><li>Promote investor education through programmes organised for school children</li><li>Provide technical assistance to adoptive financial institutions and introduce fresh ideas on investor education activities to motivate teachers and students</li></ul>
Non-governmental organisations such as consumer associations	<ul><li>Promote and create awareness of the importance of financial education programmes through the media</li><li>Publish financial education materials</li></ul>
Smart partners such as Credit Counselling and Debt Management Agency, Financial Mediation Bureau, Malaysian Deposit Insurance Corporation and relevant ministries	<ul><li>Promote public awareness of the consumer education programme targeted at school children via joint outreach programmes and dissemination of materials and create links to duitsaku.com website</li></ul>

Managing possible conflicts of interest

To mitigate possible conflicts of interest, the MoE has streamlined all the co-curricular activities conducted by private organisations for school children. As a guiding principle for heads of the 10 000 schools adopted under the SAP, financial education programmes should only be conducted by the MoE, the adoptive financial institutions and the partners of Bank Negara Malaysia. The MoE and school authorities monitor financial education activities by financial institutions to ensure that marketing activities are not conducted during financial education activities.

South Africa

From the beginning, the comprehensive implementation of the mandate for consumer education of the Financial Services Board of South Africa (FSBSA) was hampered by limited available funding sources. Given the absence of funding from own sources (besides seed money for consumer education), the FSBSA was able to develop substantial programmes through negotiated partnerships with the private financial sector.

In order to create a formal framework for the collaboration with the private sector, the FSBSA established the Financial Services Consumer Education Foundation (the Foundation) in 2004. The Foundation is an independent trust governed by trustees as a separate entity with assets separate from that of the FSBSA. The function and purpose of the Foundation is to serve as a useful vehicle for donor support to assist the FSBSA in fulfilling its consumer financial education responsibilities.

In particular, the Foundation:

- funds, promotes or otherwise supports consumer financial education, awareness, confidence and knowledge regarding consumer rights, financial products, institutions and services supervised and regulated by the FSBSA;

- promotes the use of regulated financial services, by those who do not yet avail themselves of the financial products and services available, including the poor and needy;

- educates pension fund trustees to promote the responsible management of pension funds and protection of pension fund members;

- educates financial services providers on consumer protection; and

- promotes the education and information of consumers, pension fund trustees and financial services providers so as to serve the needs, interests and well-being of the general public in the field of financial services.

The Foundation has been approved as a public benefit organisation in terms of the Income Tax Act. It is also registered as a non-profit organisation. The establishment of the Foundation made available additional funding (albeit limited) in response to proposals submitted to the Foundation by the FSBSA.

Besides this initiative, the approval of the Financial Sector Charter 1 (FSC) in 2004 further complemented the FSBSA's efforts to educate consumers. A voluntary charter was signed by key players in the financial sector, committing them to the expenditure of 0.2 percent of their after tax profits for consumer education. More recently, in 2013 the Financial Sector Codes have introduced a mandatory requirement on the financial industry to invest 0.2% of after-tax profits in consumer education activities, with the percentage set to increase to 0.4% by 2015.

United Kingdom

Private sector funding is provided directly by individual financial institutions, and indirectly through the Money Advice Service (MAS). MAS is funded entirely by a statutory levy on the financial services industry, raised through the Financial Conduct Authority (FCA), and it is leading the National Strategy for Financial Capability. As part of this strategy, MAS has notably funded pfeg's "Learning Money Matters" programme. Before MAS, the FSA was also funding this programme (with up to £1.9 million in 2009/10) and also contributed to financial education development officer posts in Wales, Scotland and Northern Ireland to ensure resources were coordinated and freely and easily available to teachers and schools. The FSA also funded research in 2006 that explored the way that financial education was being taught in schools.

As well as contributing indirectly through the FCA levy, a number of private sector financial institutions make a direct contribution to schools. An independent report for MAS, published in 2012, found that the financial services industry funded financial education for around £25 million annually in 36 programmes, most targeted at people under the age of 18. For example, HSBC funds pfeg's "What Money Means" scheme for primary schools (£3.4m over the duration of the three year project). HSBC have committed in the past up to 10 000 of their staff to the project. These volunteers go into primary schools to work with teachers to pass on their financial expertise. Prudential, GE Money and ICAEW are among the institutions that have funded pfeg's "Use Your Expertise" project that brings together volunteers in the financial services industry with teachers in the classroom. Another example is the Royal Bank of Scotland's Moneysense programme that provides direct support to teachers in schools.

In-kind support is also provided by financial institutions through talks at school on personal finance provided by financial services industry employees. For example, in Wales, Credit Unions' staffs work with teachers and pupils on an ongoing basis. There is also significant private sector funding for the production of resource materials for schools. For example, Prudential, Standard Life and Experian have funded and produced specific financial education resources for schools.

Managing possible conflicts of interest

In the United Kingdom, the Money Advice Service will deliver a voluntary "Code of Practice" for financial education providers in winter 2013/spring 2014. For the time being, it is up to individual schools and teachers to decide on the suitability of any resource or support programme. There are a number of professional support programmes available to teachers to help them feel confident and competent in delivering personal finance to their pupils, giving them confidence to select appropriate classroom resources.

In addition, the pfeg Quality Mark, a method of quality assurance, ensures teachers have access to a range of quality assured resources that have been independently assessed by educational and financial experts. These resources:

- do not bear ads and do not market a particular business or product;

- are accurate and up to date;

- match curriculum requirements and have been carefully designed for the stated age range with learning aims and objectives;

- are easily available, adaptable and low cost;

- cover an appropriate range of financial topics and are linked to the financial literacy education framework;

- have been developed in partnership with teachers and tested in schools.

It is also important for organisations leading national efforts in financial education, like MAS today or previously the FSA (and, in the devolved nations, the Scottish Centre for Financial Education, the Welsh Financial Education Unit, and the Council for the Curriculum, Examinations and Assessment in Northern Ireland) to maintain a dialogue with key industry players providing support or resources into schools. Through an ongoing dialogue the FSA was able to make the case that any resources the firms produce need to be educational and unbiased, ensuring firms do not see this as a marketing opportunity.

Evaluation of financial education programmes

As highlighted in the INFE Guidelines in Annex A, monitoring and evaluation are essential components of the successful introduction of financial education programmes in schools. Evaluation evidence is key to improving the overall effectiveness of the programme and the accountability of the stakeholders involved.

Monitoring and evaluation should ideally focus on each stage of the programme implementation.[19] Evaluation should account for both short-term outcomes and long-term impacts and may take several forms, depending on its focus.

- One of the first important steps consists of monitoring the actual teaching of financial education, for example through case studies and oversight mechanisms that can be put in place by local or national authorities.

- The second phase consists in evaluating the relevance and impact of the programme, the learning framework and the teaching through direct feedback from involved stakeholders such as students, teachers, educational system's management, parents and the local community.

- Finally, in order to test the change in the level of financial literacy of students, their competencies might be assessed throughout the curriculum via testing in the classroom, formal examinations or by including such evaluation in national tests.

The latter example is also the preliminary step towards the longer term impact evaluation of financial education programmes in schools. Such impact can also be partly measured through baseline surveys of students' financial literacy, in order to set benchmarks and goals. The use of international survey results (such as the financial literacy assessment included in the PISA 2012 and 2015 exercises [OECD, 2013]) will add further value to this evaluation method (see Box 2.1 and also "Assessment of students' achievement" in Chapter 3).

**Box 2.1. The Financial Literacy Option in the OECD Programme
for International Student Assessment (PISA)**

The OECD Programme for International Student Assessment (PISA) began in 2000. It aims to assess the capacity of students to use their knowledge and experience in "real world" situations. The emphasis of the test is on understanding concepts and mastering skills in three areas: mathematics, reading and sciences. Around 470 000 students from 65 countries completed the fourth edition of the test in 2009. Through the Financial Literacy Option first introduced in 2012 (OECD, 2013), PISA will also test for the first time 15 year-olds on their knowledge of personal finances and ability to apply it to their financial problems.

The PISA 2012 Financial Literacy Assessment is the first large-scale international study to assess the financial literacy of young people. The dedicated framework published in 2013 is the first step in constructing this financial literacy assessment of international scope by providing an articulated plan for developing items, designing the instrument and providing a common language on financial literacy issues. This framework provides a working definition for financial literacy for youth and organises the domain around the content, processes and contexts that are relevant for the assessment of 15-year-old students.

Content areas described by the framework include money and transactions, planning and managing finances, risk and reward and financial landscape. The framework covers such mental processes as identifying financial information, analysing information in a financial context, evaluating financial issues, and applying financial knowledge and understanding. These contents and processes are applied in a number of contexts, comprising education and work, home and family, individual, and societal contexts. The assessment is illustrated with 10 sample items. Additionally, the framework discusses the relationship of financial literacy to non-cognitive skills and to both mathematics and reading literacy, and the measurement of students' financial behaviour and experience.

In 2012, 65 countries or regions have taken part in the PISA test which focuses on testing mathematics literacy. Students from 18 of these countries have also tackled problems related to financial literacy: Australia, Belgium (Flemish Community), Shanghai-China, Colombia, Croatia, Czech Republic, Estonia, France, Israel, Italy, Latvia, New Zealand, Poland, Russia, Slovak Republic, Slovenia, Spain and United States. Results for the 18 participating economies will be available in June 2014.

A second assessment of financial literacy is planned in the 2015 PISA Financial Literacy exercise, with the following volunteering countries: Australia, Belgium (Flemish Community), Brazil, Canada (some provinces), Chile, England, Italy, Lithuania, Netherlands, New Zealand, Peru, Poland, Russian Federation, Slovak Republic, Spain, and United States.

In spite of its recognised importance, evaluation of the relevance and impact of programmes (second phase) remains relatively rare, although the situation is improving. In Spain, data compiled from 2011 has been assessed in 2012-13 for adaptation of the National Strategy on Financial Education and the Netherlands has evaluated different teaching methodologies. In the province of British Columbia, Canada, there has been ongoing evaluation of the effectiveness of the financial education programme. In New Zealand, an independent evaluation of the draft financial education framework was undertaken and the findings of the evaluation were used to shape the final form of the framework. In Australia, ASIC has contracted the Australian Council of Education Research to conduct an evaluation of the teaching of the MoneySmart programme pilot phase (2012) and notably to recommend, on the basis of these findings, how to track long-term behavioural change.

Public authorities also have a role to play in pushing private sector providers to evaluate their initiatives. In the United Kingdom, the Money Advice Service will deliver a voluntary 'Code of Practice' for financial education providers in winter 2013/spring 2014. This "Code of Practice" aims to maximise the impact of industry-funded programmes, and will include an evaluation framework in order for intervention providers to assess impact and increase the body of evidence over what works.

Concerning tests on changes in the financial competencies of students (third phase), in most countries financial education is not part of student examination as a separate subject. Instead, countries are evaluating financial education as part of the already existing evaluation of the subject to which it is integrated, as in Korea where personal finance competence is tested as part of other subjects.

Some countries have however set up formal and/or informal assessment of financial education (rather than examinations). Malaysia has monthly interactive games, self-assessment quizzes and writing competitions. The United Kingdom has qualifications by the Qualifications and Curriculum Development Agency (QCA) and National Database of Accredited Qualifications (NDAQ), which contain units on personal finance education, and within the United Kingdom there have been further evaluations in Scotland (one of the early adopters of financial education in schools) undertaken by George Street Research and an evaluation of pfeg's "Learning Money Matters" programme in England undertaken by the National Foundation for Educational Research.

The case studies in this section of the report are based on the evaluations of a wide pilot project in Brazil, the Planning 10 programme in the province of British Columbia, Canada and various provisions in England and Scotland, Italy, Malaysia and South Africa.

Brazil shows the benefits of evaluating a pilot programme ahead of a nation-wide implementation. British Columbia is an example of a monitoring exercise used to strengthen the effectiveness of financial education programmes and to inform the development of further programmes. England illustrates the need not only to count the number of schools effectively engaging in financial education, but also to understand whether this sample is representative of the overall educational system. Italy provides interesting insights into knowledge retention gauged through tests repeated over several years of financial education. Malaysia provides an interesting example of evaluation in a context characterised by a strong involvement of the private sector where financial institutions serve both as providers of content and as channels for monitoring and testing results. Scotland is a useful example of a two-stage evaluation that included a survey of the adoption of financial education programmes in different sectors of the educational system and secondly an analysis of the perception of their effectiveness. Finally South Africa shows how to develop guidelines for evaluation and a toolkit and how to make their use compulsory in all financial education programmes.

Brazil

The introduction of financial education in schools is part of the Brazilian National Strategy on Financial Education (ENEF). In 2010, Brazil introduced a pilot programme for financial education in high-schools and to measure the impact of the programme with the support of the Russian Trust Fund on Financial Literacy and Education and the World Bank[20] before scaling it up in other parts of the country. This pilot followed two years of preparation to develop guidelines, the first materials and the implementation plan.

The schools programme integrates financial education within the school curriculum and incorporates case studies on financial literacy into mathematics, language/literature, science, sociology and other disciplines. In the State of São Paulo, for example, there were schools that chose to include the financial content into five different disciplines at the same time.

The pilot study design was based on random assignment. Schools that volunteered to be part of the programme were randomly selected to be either in the "treatment group" or the "control group". The randomisation was done at the school level and divided the pilot study sample into two groups: a treatment groups that received both textbooks and teacher training, and a control group. In order to also gauge the potential effects on parents, half of the parents in treatment schools were randomly selected to participate in a parent financial education workshop.

In total 891 schools in six states (439 treatment and 452 control schools) and approximately 26 000 students (one class per school) participated in the evaluation of the pilot.

Box 2.2. Timeline of the Brazilian evaluation of financial education in schools

- April–May 2010: the list of interested schools was determined with help of the different State Ministries of Education. Once the volunteers sample put together, they were randomly divided into treatment and control group.

- May–July 2010: teacher training began.

- Early August 2010: baseline survey conducted.

- Mid-August 2010: Teachers began teaching the material developed by the working group (until November 2011).

- Late November 2010: First follow-up survey (following one semester of financial education).

- Spring/Summer 2011: Parent workshops.

- November 2011: Second follow-up survey.

- July 2013: Evaluation results published.

The random assignment method helped determine whether the school-based financial education programme led to changes in financial knowledge, attitudes, and decision-making. The outcomes of interest were at the student level and at the family level.

The evaluation included three instruments: a financial literacy test, a students' questionnaire, and a parents' questionnaire. These three instruments were specifically designed for the production of various measures: the measure of financial literacy, the extent of autonomy of students on financial matters and the level of intention to save.

The results are very encouraging (Bruhn et al, forthcoming). The follow-up surveys demonstrated that the average level of financial proficiency is higher in the treatment group than in the control group. The same is true for the level of financial autonomy and for the attitude to savings. All effects are statistically significant (at 1% level in most cases). There were also positive effects on parents. The evaluation found an increase in parental financial knowledge, in the discussion of financial matters within families and a higher number of families drafting a household budget.

The policy implications of the pilot are considerable. The Ministry of Education has decided to scale up the programme to the 5 000 Brazilian high schools, and to pilot a programme for primary schools. It was also decided to develop a virtual platform for national dissemination of resources and the further development of guidance. Finally, depending on feasibility, students will be tracked over time after leaving school using the national identification number (CPF).

The Province of British Columbia (BC), Canada

British Columbia has a financial literacy course as part of its core curriculum. Developed by the British Columbia Securities Commission (BCSC), the goal of the "Planning 10" course is to give students the financial life-skills they need as adults. It was introduced into schools in 2005 and in the same year, it received Provincially Recommended status from the BC Ministry of Education. The BCSC has undertaken an ongoing programme to monitor the use and effectiveness of their Planning 10 financial education course and the Planning 10 Teacher Resource.

Working with a survey company, the BCSC designed an email survey to gather teachers' feedback on their use and rating of the "Planning 10" resources in the 2004-2005 school years. The survey was repeated the following year. The following are key findings from the comparison of the survey data across the two years:

- Resource use increased 14 percent.
- Overall positive resource rating increased slightly.
- Overall use of resource materials decreased slightly.
- Student use of the resource increased by 30 percent.

BCSC are using the data from these surveys as a guide to update and refresh the resource.

In the summer of 2006, the BCSC worked with a research company to design pre- and post- tests to gather student feedback about "Planning 10". Students were asked to indicate their responses to questions both before and after being exposed to the "Planning 10" course materials. Forty-two students were divided into two classes and were taught "Planning 10": Finances over four days. Key findings from the research were:

- The majority of students found the topics interesting, engaging and easy to understand.
- 85% rated the course "B" or higher.
- Students were most likely to use the financial life skills topic and vulnerability to fraud.

To gather further feedback from students about the "Planning 10" resource, the BCSC also conducted a student focus-group in one of the province's high schools. Students were asked about the key characters in the student resource and the feedback has been used to inform the ongoing development of the resource.

BCSC undertook two high school graduate outcome surveys with one school district in BC in 2007 and 2008. For the past 14 years, this school district had assessed high school graduates (two years after they've graduated) on the following:

- whether or not the graduates had gained employment;
- whether or not they had gone on to post-secondary education or training;
- whether or not their school learning and experiences had prepared them for life, work and further education.

In previous surveys, the graduates did not feel that their high school education had prepared them enough to manage their finances. To assess the recent graduates' current financial life skills and whether their high school experience had prepared them to manage their finances, the 2007 survey added thirteen questions. The BCSC developed these questions in consultation with the research firm and the school district. By surveying recent high school graduates, the BCSC wanted to find out if young adults in BC were becoming more financially literate as a result of taking the mandatory Planning 10 Finances course.

The methodology involved the use of current high school students to conduct the survey with recent graduates as the school district found that the graduates were more responsive when being surveyed by students. Key findings were that the 2008 graduates learned more about managing their finances than 2006 graduates. The researchers concluded that Planning 10 Finances, taken by the 2008 graduates, may account for this increased learning. The BCSC considers this survey as longitudinal research and plans to continue to work with the school district on surveying graduates and finding out how they are managing their financial lives.

For the past five years, BCSC has also been tracking the use of Planning 10 website. The evaluation of Planning 10 by the BCSC has provided ongoing evidence of the effectiveness of the resource. This was important in influencing the Financial Consumer Agency of Canada (FCAC) when it was reviewing financial education initiatives across Canada to identify successful programmes. On the strength of the evidence of the success of Planning 10, FCAC partnered with the BCSC to build on this initiative and extend it across Canada in a resource called "The City".

England, United Kingdom

The National Foundation for Educational Research (NFER) has undertaken an independent evaluation of the Learning Money Matters (LMM) initiative on behalf of the Personal Financial Education Group (pfeg). LMM provides help, support and advice for secondary schools in England in delivering personal financial education (PFE) to their students. The evaluation report was released in September 2009.

Methods

The evaluation design was based on four methods:

- an analysis of the pfeg database to identify how representative the secondary schools who participate in the initiative are of all secondary schools in England;

- two telephone surveys with sample schools to gain a broad picture of the effectiveness and impact of LMM;

- case-study visits to selected schools; and

- telephone interviews with pfeg consultants.

Evaluation findings

The following key findings are quoted directly from the evaluation report (Spielhofer et al, 2009).

- The research underlines the ongoing need in schools for the support provided by pfeg through LMM. Delivery of Personal and Financial Education (PFE) remains variable across schools, with many schools not yet delivering lessons to students in all year groups in an effective way. Furthermore, 3 690 schools and colleges – that is over 53 per cent of all providers – had not yet been involved in LMM by the end of June 2009.

- The majority of teachers are very satisfied with the support provided by pfeg consultants. They particularly value consultants' knowledge of financial topics, resources and curriculum requirements, their professionalism and their flexibility in responding to the needs of the school and students.

- Involvement in LMM often acts as a catalyst to encourage teachers to initiate or expand the teaching of PFE in their schools. However, this encouragement needs to be supported within schools by senior management buy-in, sufficient curriculum time and enthusiastic and motivated teaching staff in order to ensure the successful and sustained delivery of PFE.

- The main barriers to the successful delivery of PFE in schools include other competing curriculum demands, lack of time to prepare and coordinate delivery, and difficulties in finding staff that are interested, confident and enthusiastic about teaching PFE.

- PFE lessons have a noticeable impact on students' attitudes towards saving and borrowing, their confidence in dealing with money and their views on being taught about finance at school. The study also identified an impact on students' knowledge of finance and financial products in some schools.

The evaluation report provides recommendations for actions based on the key findings. These are that:

- ongoing support is provided to schools involved in LMM;

- ways to foster and strengthen ongoing commitment to PFE within schools be considered;

- promoting the value and importance of PFE to all schools and colleges; and

- developing a good practice guide that consultants can share with schools.

"The study has shown that LMM has encouraged many schools to make considerable progress towards implementing a stronger platform for PFE learning, in particular, by helping them to develop appropriate teaching approaches and resources. However, it has also highlighted that more needs to be done not only to sustain and improve the teaching of PFE in existing LML schools, but also to extend and embed effectively to a broader range of schools. There is a danger that without the continued support provided by pfeg, through initiatives such as LMM, that the gains made in securing a PFE entitlement for all students in schools will be lost" (Spielhofer, et al. 2009).

Italy

In the 2008-09 school years, the Bank of Italy and the Italian Ministry of Education (MIUR) implemented an experimental programme to incorporate financial education into school curricula, in the last two years of each school level: Grades 4 and 5 in primary school, Grades 7 and 8 in junior high school and Grades 12 and 13 in high school. The programme was piloted in the school year 2008/09 on 631 students from 32 classes in three regions of the country. It was then made available nationwide, with the number of participating schools increasing every year. In school year 2011/12 the programme was implemented in 1.150 classes and financial education taught to 23 000 students.

Participation to the programme is voluntary, and financial education is introduced with a cross-curricular approach. Interested teachers receive training from Bank of Italy's officials, focusing in particular on money and transactions. At the beginning of each school year, MIUR presents the programme and schools decide whether to participate or not, and which classes could be included. The Bank then supplies teachers with appropriate training and pedagogical resources.

The training, which includes lectures from specialists from the Bank of Italy, aims both at increasing the awareness of the importance of financial literacy and at developing confidence among teachers. In order to further assist teachers who might not be familiar with the matters, the Bank of Italy has developed pedagogic material tailored to the needs of the different age groups and relevant teachers' guides.

As recommended by the INFE High-level Principles for the Evaluation of Financial Education Programmes (INFE 2011), the programme has included evaluation since its design. The evaluation focused on students' knowledge, and was undertaken through tests administered to pupils before and after classroom teaching (Romagnoli and Trifilidis, 2013). An increase in financial knowledge was defined as the gain in scores or the difference in the percentage of correct answers between post-classroom teaching and pre-classroom teaching tests. The tests were differentiated by school level for both effort and duration. Although the Bank of Italy-MIUR programme lacked a formal control group, having tests administered to all participants allowed the identification of specific subsamples to examine the robustness of the findings and knowledge retention over time.

The sample also allowed for the evaluation of longer-term retention of financial knowledge. Participants from 2011-12 could be split into two subsamples: those involved during the first year and those involved in the follow-up. Since the follow-up group had covered the core issue during the previous school year, pre-testing results on the core topic that were different from those of the peer group indicated knowledge retention.

Indeed, the continuing pupils showed significantly higher levels of knowledge than their coevals. As the tests were different from those of the previous edition, this was consistent with the fact that some of the information learned was retained after one year and it confirmed the effectiveness of the programme in increasing students' knowledge.

The evaluation also allowed identifying a gender gap in financial knowledge. Testing prior to classroom teaching showed female students scoring lower than male ones in all age groups. This gap was reduced following classroom teaching. In the case of junior high-schools, female students scored better than male ones in the post treatment tests.

Given the robustness of the results obtained through the repeated evaluation of students' knowledge, the Bank of Italy and MIUR have decided to momentarily suspend testing of students, in order to devote more resources to the teachers' survey.

Malaysia

The evaluation of financial literacy programmes for children in Malaysia is conducted through pre and post-training surveys at workshops for children. The primary aim of the evaluation is to assess the programme for its appropriateness and effectiveness. This is to ensure that the programme objectives meet the needs of the participants.

The collection of information and data takes place in two stages: through a pre-workshop questionnaire administered prior to the commencement of the workshop and through a post-workshop questionnaire - aimed to reflect the change in children's levels of satisfaction with the programme and the appropriateness and effectiveness of programme content.

Awareness of the financial education programme in schools as well as among students is also measured based on the analysis of the number of hits on the financial education website (duitsaku.com) and a count of members. Evaluation also takes place through the assessment of students using the Pocket Money Book to manage their daily finances.

Moreover, as Malaysia benefits from strong partnership between public sector and financial institutions (FIs), the evaluation of programmes and of their effectiveness is also done by monitoring the level of involvement and activity of the private sector. In particular, useful data are collected by analysing the frequency of visits made by FIs to their adopted schools; the percentage of FIs distributing the Pocket Money Book and of those briefing students on the use and importance of the Pocket Money Book; and finally the percentage of FIs conducting competitions on the use of the Pocket Money Book.

Scotland, United Kingdom

The Scottish Government commissioned in September 2009 an independent evaluation of financial education in primary and secondary schools[21]. The evaluation was commissioned by the Curriculum division, part of the Schools Directorate within the Scottish Government. Scotland was the first country in the United Kingdom to develop financial education initiatives beginning in 1999 with "Financial Education in Scottish Schools: A Statement of Position".[22] From 2008 onwards, financial education has been a cross-curricular activity that all schools have been required to address. However, the Government recognised that very little was known about the impacts of financial education and the effectiveness and outcomes for young people as a result of their engagement with financial education programmes in schools.

Methods

The evaluation design was based on two phases. The first phase involved identifying and collating available information and research on the range and penetration of financial education programmes across different Curriculum stages in primary and secondary schools. Existing research evidence about the effectiveness of different forms of financial education in Scotland was also reviewed.

The second phase of the evaluation investigated the perceptions of the effectiveness of financial education programmes and resources from teacher, head teacher and student perspectives. Evaluation methods used were online surveys, qualitative interviews in selected schools with teachers, head teachers and students and stakeholder interviews and consultation with relevant policy makers, providers and interested parties.

Evaluation findings

The evaluation showed that financial education programmes were being delivered by the large majority of respondent schools across a wide range of subject areas and student ages. However, while financial education is intended to be taught as a cross-curricular activity, it was being delivered largely through special activities rather than integrated into a range of lessons across the curriculum.

The evaluation identified a number of barriers to the inclusion of financial education in schools. These included the low status and priority accorded to financial education in secondary schools and the lack of co-ordination, communication and organisation across departments in secondary schools. Lack of teaching time and resources were identified as barriers as well as a lack of investment by schools in budget or staff time into teacher training in financial education.

Support from local authority staff and other stakeholder organisations and leadership and support from head teachers were identified as supporting factors for the inclusion of financial education. Teachers and students identified key aspects related to the effectiveness of financial education in schools. These were:

- interactivity;
- teaching resources and worksheets;
- examples such as stories and realistic examples that students can relate to;
- information on how to run events such as Money Week;
- real life examples that are relevant and practical;
- external support, help and advice.

The evaluation makes a number of recommendations about ways to strengthen the provision and effectiveness of financial education in Scottish schools. Best-practice examples and case studies of the effective delivery of financial education across primary and secondary schools will be developed based on the evaluation findings.

South Africa

In 2008, the Financial Services Board of South Africa (FSBSA) commissioned research on the development of a framework to monitor and facilitate the effective delivery of financial literacy programmes in South Africa. The report, published in February 2009, highlights the complex nature of monitoring and evaluating financial education programmes. The research further underscores the need to understand and assess financial behaviour within the context of local constraints, not least of which is the availability of suitable financial products and services.

From the research, the FSBSA developed the "Guidelines for monitoring and evaluating consumer financial education programmes". The purpose of this document is to provide organisations that offer financial education programmes with a set of guidelines or a "toolkit" for monitoring and evaluating these programmes. It is compulsory for all programmes and projects of the FSBSA relating to financial education to have a monitoring and evaluation strategy. In 2011, the FSBSA conducted a national baseline study to determine financial literacy levels in South Africa. Currently, the FSBSA is developing monitoring and evaluation process in line with the baseline study. These processes will apply to all programmes, including those targeted at schools and teachers.

Notes

1. Australian Ministerial Council, now called the Ministerial Council for Education, Early Childhood Education and Youth Affairs (MCEECDYA), is the vehicle for coordinating strategic education policy at the national level in Australia, including negotiation of national priorities based on shared objectives and interests. The members of MCEECDYA include State, Territory, Australian Government and New Zealand Ministers with responsibility for the portfolios of school education, early childhood development and youth affairs.

2. http://www.mceecdya.edu.au/mceecdya/national_goals_for_schooling_working_group, 24776.html

3. See http://www.acara.edu.au/curriculum/curriculum.html

4. See www.acara.edu.au

5. For more information on the Brazilian National Strategy, please see Russia's G20 Presidency/OECD, 2013.

6. See nzcurriculum.tki.org.nz/Curriculum-resources/Learning-and-teaching-resources/Financial-capability

7. Financial Services Authority of the UK (2006).

8. Financial Services Authority of the UK (2006).

9. The school stories are available at the following link: nzcurriculum.tki.org.nz/Curriculum-resources/Learning-and-teaching-resources/Financial-capability/FC-school-stories

10. www.nicurriculum.org.uk/fc/

11. More information available at www.pfeg.org/curriculum_and_policy/northern_ireland/index.html and www.nicurriculum.org.uk/fc/

12. The following web-link provides an example of the draft overview www.nicurriculum.org.uk/microsite/financial_capability/documents/keystage1/FC_S pec_key_stage_1.pdf

13. www.themoneybelt.gc.ca

14. www.pfeg.org/teaching_resources/index.html

15. Jump$tart Coalition for Personal Financial Literacy (2007).

16. The OECD/INFE is currently developing Guidelines for Private and Civil Stakeholders in Financial Education, to be finalised in 2014.

17. www.duitsaku.com

18. Guides and lesson plans available at www.duitaksu.com

19. See also INFE (2011) and Yoong et al., 2013

20. The Pilot evaluation was made possible by the collaboration between several institutions within the framework of the activities of the Russian/World Bank/OECD Trust Fund on Financial Literacy. The collaborating institutions are the World Bank Research Department and DIME, Centro de Políticas Públicas e Avaliação da Educação

(CAEd) together with private sector organisations such as Associação Brasileira das Entidades dos Mercados Financeiro e de Capitais (ANBIMA), BM&F BOVESPA, Federação Brasileira de Bancos (FEBRABAN), and Institute Unibanco (IU).

21.   Scottish Government Social Research, (2009).

22.   Learning Teaching Scotland (1999).

References

OECD Recommendations

OECD (2005), Recommendation on Principles and Good Practices on Financial Education and Awareness.
http://www.oecd.org/finance/financial-education/35108560.pdf

OECD/INFE instruments and relevant outputs

Atkinson, A. and F-A Messy, (2012), Measuring Financial Literacy: Results of the OECD/INFE Pilot Study, *OECD Working Papers on Finance, Insurance and Private Pensions,* No. 15, OECD Publishing, http://dx.doi.org/10.1787/5k9csfs90fr4-en

Grifoni, A. and F-A Messy, (2012), Current Status of National Strategies for Financial Education: a Comparative Analysis and Relevant Practices, *Working Papers on Finance, Insurance and Private Pensions,* No. 16, OECD Publishing, http://dx.doi.org/10.1787/5k9bcwct7xmn-en

OECD/INFE (2009), Financial Education and the Crisis: Policy Paper and Guidance, www.oecd.org/finance/financial-education/50264221.pdf

INFE (2010a), Guide to Evaluating Financial Education Programmes, available at *www.financial-education.org.*

INFE (2010b), Detailed Guide to Evaluating Financial Education Programmes, available at *www.financial-education.org.*

INFE (2011), High-level Principles for the Evaluation of Financial Education Programmes,
available at *www.financial-education.org.*

OECD/INFE (2012), High-level Principles on National Strategy for Financial Education, available at:
www.oecd.org/finance/financialeducation/OECD_INFE_High_Level_Principles_Nati onal_Strategies_Financial_Education_APEC.pdf

OECD/INFE (2013), Toolkit to Measure Financial Literacy and Inclusion: *Guidance, Core Questionnaire and Supplementary Questions.* available at *www.financial-education.org.*

OECD (2013), "Financial Literacy Framework", in OECD, PISA 2012 Assessment and Analytical Framework: Mathematics, Reading, Science, Problem Solving and Financial Literacy, OECD Publishing. doi: 10.1787/9789264190511-7-en

Other references

Bruhn, M., L. de Souza Leao, A. Legovini, R. Marchetti, B. Zia, (2014, forthcoming), "Financial Education and Behaviour Formation: Large-Scale Experimental Evidence from Brazil", World Bank.

COREMEC, Comitê de Regulação e Fiscalização dos Mercados Financeiro, de Capitais, de Seguros, de Previdência e Capitalização, (2009a), Estratégia Nacional de Educação Financeira, available at
www.vidaedinheiro.gov.br/Imagens/Plano%20Diretor%20ENEF.pdf

COREMEC, Comitê de Regulação e Fiscalização dos Mercados Financeiro, de Capitais, de Seguros, de Previdência e Capitalização (2009b), "Orientação para Educação Financeira nas Escolas", *Estratégia Nacional de Educação Financeira – Anexos,* available at *www.vidaedinheiro.gov.br/Imagens/Plano%20Diretor%20ENEF%20-%20anexos.pdf*

Financial Services Authority of the UK (2006), Financial Capability in the UK, Creating a Step Change in Schools, available at *www.fsa.gov.uk/pubs/other/step_change.pdf*

Jump$tart Coalition for Personal Financial Literacy (2007), National Standards in K–12 Personal Finance Education with Benchmarks, Knowledge Statements, and Glossary, available at *www.jumpstart.org/assets/files/standard_book-ALL.pdf*

Learning Teaching Scotland (1999), Financial Education in Scottish Schools: A Statement of Position, available at
www.ltscotland.org.uk/Images/financialedstatement_tcm4-121478.pdf

Learning Teaching Scotland (2010), Financial Education: Developing Skills for Learning, Life and Work, available at
http://www.educationscotland.gov.uk/Images/developing_skills_web_tcm4-639212.pdf

Learning Teaching Scotland (2010), Maintaining Momentum: a Partnership Approach to Improving Financial Education in Scottish Schools, available at *www.educationscotland.gov.uk/publications/m/publication_tcm4639238.asp*

Romagnoli A. and Trifilidis M. (2013), Does financial education at school work? Evidence from Italy, *Occasional Papers (Questioni di Economia e Finanza),* No 155, Bank of Italy Publishing.

Russia's G20 Presidency – OECD (2013), Advancing National Strategies for Financial Education, available at http://www.oecd.org/finance/financial-education/G20_OECD_NSFinancialEducation.pdf

Government Social Research (2009), Evaluation of Financial Education in Scottish Primary and Secondary Schools, available at
www.scotland.gov.uk/Resource/Doc/259782/0077311.pdf

Spielhofer T., D. Kerr and C. Gardiner (2009), Evaluation of Learning Money Matters. Final Report, National Foundation for Educational Research, available at *www.nfer.ac.uk/nfer/publications/LMM01/LMM01.pdf*

Yoong, A., K. Mihaly, S. Bauhoff, L. Rabinovich, and A. Hung (2013), A toolkit for the Evaluation of Financial Capability Programs in Low- and Middle-Income Countries, www.finlitedu.org/team-downloads/evaluation/toolkit-for-the-evaluation-of-financial-capability-programs-in-low-and-middle-income-countries.pdf

Chapter 3

Comparing selected financial education learning frameworks

Learning frameworks provide a planned and coherent structure for financial education in the official school sector, at the primary or secondary level. They operate at meta-level, providing learning outcomes or standards for financial education. This chapter illustrates the INFE Guidance on Learning Frameworks that complement the INFE Guidelines displayed in Annex A. It provides both a comparative analysis of the learning frameworks, from their design to their practical implementation, and a detailed description of available relevant frameworks. The analysis focuses first on their development, and notably on the institutions responsible for their drafting, the goals and institutional endorsement. It then addresses their content, from the dimensions of financial education they focus on to the learning outcomes and topics, and their implementation, including links with other subjects, effective pedagogy, students' assessment and the role of teachers.

Scope and definition

For the purposes of this analysis, learning frameworks were defined as those that provided a planned and coherent framework for financial education for the official school sector at a national level (or significantly locally and regionally). A learning or curriculum framework operates at a meta-level, providing learning outcomes or standards for financial education over the compulsory school sector, or the primary or secondary level. Eleven financial education curriculum/learning frameworks met these criteria and were included in the analysis on which this report is based.

This chapter is articulated around two sections. The first part provides a comparative analysis of the learning frameworks in relation to their institutional organisational features and their content and pedagogical features. The second part provides an overview of each of the frameworks in relation to their key features.

Table 3.1 Summary of learning frameworks on financial education

Country	Framework	Date Published	Responsible Institutions
Australia	National Consumer and Financial Literacy Framework	First published 2005 Updated 2009, 2011	Ministerial Council for Education, Early Childhood and Development and Youth Affairs (MCEECDYA)
Brazil	Guidance for Financial Education in Schools	2009	Department of Education at national and local levels; coordinated by the Brazilian Security Exchange Commission (CVM) with the support of the Central Bank, the Private Pension Plans Secretary (PREVUC) and the Insurance Supervisory and Regulatory Authority (SUSEP)
England 2008*	Guidance on Financial Capability in the Secondary Curriculum: Key Stage 3 and 4	2008	Department for Children, Schools and Families
Japan	Financial Education Programme	2007	Central Council for Financial Services Information
Netherlands	Basic Vision on financial education: curriculum framework for development and implementation	January 2009	Money Wise Platform headed by the Dutch Ministry of Finance
Malaysia	Framework on Financial Education for Malaysian school children under the School Adoption Programme	2006	Bank Negara Malaysia, in collaboration with the Ministry of Education and the financial institutions that participate in the Schools Adoption programme
New Zealand	Financial Capability in the Curriculum	2009	The Ministry of Education with input from the Commission for Financial Literacy and Retirement Income
Northern Ireland	Northern Ireland Curriculum Financial Capability	2007	Northern Ireland Executive, Council for the Curriculum, Examinations and Assessment
Scotland	Financial Education in Scottish Schools; A Statement of Position	1999	Scottish Council of Consultative Council on the Curriculum
South Africa	Integrated in the SA National Curriculum Statement	2004 2010 (revised)	Department of Education and Financial Services Board
USA-Jump$tart	National Standards in K-12 Personal Financial Education	3rd Edition, 2007	Jump$tart Coalition for Personal Financial Literacy

* This curriculum is kept for useful reference but it is not currently taught due to developments within the United Kingdom.

History of the development of existing frameworks

In Scotland, New Zealand, Northern Ireland and England the financial education frameworks were developed by government education agencies with responsibility for the school curriculum. In Australia, the development of the framework was commissioned by the Australian Government's Ministerial Council on Education, Training and Youth Affairs (MCEETYA) which is made up of representatives from all state and territorial jurisdictions. In South Africa, the learning framework was developed by the Department of Education and the Financial Services Board.

In Malaysia, Japan and the Netherlands there was significant private sector input into the development of the learning frameworks. Bank Negara Malaysia collaborated with the Ministry of Education and other financial institutions to take a leadership role in the financial education framework. In Japan, the Central Council for Financial Services Information, comprised of the Bank of Japan and other member organisations, took a lead role in the development of the financial education programme. In the Netherlands, an agreement was concluded by the government and partners from the financial sector and consumer organisations.

The framework from the United States was developed by the Jump$tart Coalition for Personal Financial Literacy, a not-for-profit organisation consisting of 180 private sector and educational organisations and 47 affiliated state coalitions. It does not cover mandatorily the national school system.

In Brazil, New Zealand, South Africa and the United Kingdom government-funded agencies with responsibility for national leadership of financial education strategies took a leading role in initiating and developing the financial education frameworks. In New Zealand, the Commission for Financial Literacy and Retirement Income developed, trialled and independently evaluated the draft framework then formally handed responsibility to the Ministry of Education. The Financial Services Board of South Africa played a significant role in developing the financial education component which was integrated in the National Curriculum Statement (NCS). In the United Kingdom, the Financial Services Authority and the Government set out a joint action plan for financial literacy. This work created the impetus and informed the development of the frameworks for England and Northern Ireland.

Framework goals and endorsement

In Australia, England, Japan, the Netherlands, New Zealand, Northern Ireland, Scotland and South Africa, the goals of the frameworks are similar. They aim to provide guidance directly to schools and teachers to encourage and support them to understand financial education and to incorporate it into their teaching and learning programmes. In the Netherlands, guidance is also provided for parents.

In contrast, because of their federal education policies and state education systems, the frameworks Brazil and the United States are aimed at providing guidance at the state level in the development of their curricular for financial education, and as such, no specific curricular links are provided. Both of these frameworks also aim to provide guidance to developers of instructional materials for financial education. In Brazil, a working group composed of different government agencies set up a pedagogical support group with representatives from state and local governments in order to produce a strategic document for financial education at schools.

In Malaysia, the current framework aims to provide a guide to teachers but also to the financial institutions that develop financial education programmes under the auspices of the School Adoption Programme.

With the exception of the Jump$tart framework, all of the frameworks have been endorsed by the respective government education authorities in each jurisdiction. The Jump$tart framework has not been officially endorsed, but it has been subject to ongoing review and has been adopted by the majority of financial education providers in the United States as a framework for a personal education curriculum.

Comparative analysis of content and pedagogical features

What is the focus for financial education and how is this defined?

The Australian and Malaysian frameworks focus on the development of "financial literacy", whereas the Australian and Dutch definitions also include consumer literacy. The New Zealand, English, Scottish and Northern Ireland financial literacy frameworks' focus is named "financial capability". In South Africa, the financial education component integrated in different courses (economic and management sciences, mathematical literacy, consumer studies and accounting) encompasses a mix of financial knowledge and understanding, skills, attitudes/responsibilities and behaviours. The Japanese framework focuses on financial education which includes "pecuniary education".

While different terms are used for the focus of the financial education frameworks, there are strong similarities in the definitions for the terms. In all cases, financial literacy and financial capability are seen as being more than being able to make calculations about money. Both are seen as competencies involving knowledge and skills and the ability to use these to make effective financial decisions (see table 3.1.3 in Appendix 3.A1). In this chapter, the term financial literacy is used except when discussing the name of a framework.

For countries using the term "financial capability", this is defined as the ability to make informed decisions about the personal use and management of money. In Northern Ireland, financial capability also encompasses the notion of financial responsibility. In England, a financially capable person is defined as someone who is a confident, questioning and informed consumer of financial services. The Scottish framework, like the Australian, includes the impact of financial decisions on people's lives but also on the wider environment in the definition of financial capability.

"Financial literacy" is also seen as encompassing behaviours, knowledge, understanding and skills. Definitions of financial literacy in the United States and Malaysia focus solely on the individual level. In contrast, the Australian definition takes a broader view, encompassing consumer literacy and the impact on the environment and the wider society through ethical decision making.

"Consumer and financial literacy is the application of knowledge, understandings, skills and values in consumer and financial contexts and the related decisions that impact on self, others, the community and the environment." [1]

The Japanese framework focuses on understanding money and finance with the aim of producing values and attitudes that will result in individual life style improvement as well as wider social improvement.

Dimensions of financial education

The frameworks include similar dimensions of financial education. These are financial knowledge and understanding; financial skills and competence and attitudes and/or values. The Scottish, Australian, Japanese and South African frameworks also include enterprise as a dimension of financial education.

In their attitudes and values dimension, the Australian, New Zealand, Malaysian, South African, Scottish and Northern Ireland frameworks include recognition of the wider community and/or the environment. For example, the Malaysian framework includes the dimension of financial responsibility to enable children to appreciate how financial decisions can impact on an individual, their family and the community. The Dutch framework focuses also on social financial competences such as sustainable investments, and the Brazilian one encompasses the economy and the financial systems/banks.

In the English 2008 and Jump$tart frameworks, the attitudes and values are more limited in scope and focus only on personal responsibility without referring to the wider impact of personal financial behaviours.

The dimensions of the Japanese framework are focused on the development of financial understanding at an individual level and include consumer rights and careers education.

Learning outcomes/standards

All of the frameworks provide learning outcomes or standards. However, there is some variation in the ways these are presented.

With the exception of Malaysia and Scotland, the frameworks provide specific learning outcomes that are based on progressions of learning across curriculum levels. These are typically organised according to the dimensions of financial education. The Malaysian and Scottish frameworks provide a description or list of learning outcomes for each dimension, but these are not levelled. The South African framework provides a list of learning outcomes per subject in which financial literacy is integrated depending on grade level. The Dutch framework provides a detailed list of key concepts in financial literacy according to age and sector (with a distinction between general and vocational-oriented learning targets).

Topics/issues covered

The frameworks have a number of topics in common. These are:

- money and transaction;
- planning and managing finances (including saving and spending; credit and debt; financial decision-making);
- risk and rewards;
- financial landscape (including consumers' rights and responsibilities and understanding of the wider financial, economic and social system).

Australia, Japan, Northern Ireland, Scotland and South Africa also include consumer rights and responsibilities. The Jump$tart, Japanese, Malaysian and South African frameworks include investment. The South African framework also encompasses caution against scams as well as recourse, insurance and retirement.

Levels covered

The Dutch, Japanese, Malaysian, Scottish and Jump$tart frameworks cover the whole of the formal school sector. The Australian, New Zealand, and Northern Ireland frameworks cover kindergarten or the beginning of primary school to Year 10 (early secondary level). The Scottish and English 2008 frameworks focus on the secondary level only, up to Key Stage 4. The South African framework covers grade 7-12.

Approach to inclusion of financial education in the curriculum (see also "Implementing financial education in schools" in Chapter 2)

In all of the frameworks, a cross-curricular and/or integrated approach is recommended as a way to include financial education in teaching and learning programmes. In most cases, this is because the learning outcomes for financial education are not explicitly included in existing curricular subjects.

The English curriculum from 2008 is something of an exception as financial literacy is explicitly included within personal, social, health and economic education (PSHE) at secondary level in the economic wellbeing and financial literacy programmes of study. However, the English 2008 framework also recommends an integrated curriculum approach for the inclusion of financial education learning outcomes within other subjects.

The Jump$tart framework recommends either a curriculum integrated approach or designing new financial education courses depending on which approach is most appropriate for the specific context at state level.

Curriculum links

The Dutch, English, Japanese, New Zealand, Northern Ireland, Scottish and South African frameworks provide specific links between the financial education learning outcomes and the learning outcomes in specific curricular subjects. This also applies to the implementation plan envisaged by the Dutch framework. Links are not included in the Australian and Jump$tart frameworks because they operate within a federal education system where curricular links need to be made at the state and local level.

The following subjects are recommended as suitable vehicles for integration of financial education (in order of frequency):

- living skills; personal and social development; personal, social, health and economic education; citizenship; environment and society; moral education; social and vocational skills;
- mathematics and numeracy;
- national language programmes; literacy; modern languages;
- science; environmental studies;
- economics; business management; accounting;
- social and consumer studies;
- geography;
- the Arts;
- design and technology; information communications technology (ICT); craft and design;
- religious education;
- modern studies.

The Australian and New Zealand framework make explicit links to over-arching curriculum achievement objectives such as the development of key competencies and values and recommends financial literacy as a theme that schools could use for cross-curricular teaching and learning.

The Scottish and English frameworks also refer to the relevance of financial education to meeting over-arching curriculum objectives. For example, the English framework cites the three statutory aims of the secondary curriculum and states that financial education contributes to all three aims, as follows:

- successful learners who enjoy learning, make progress and achieve;
- confident individuals who are able to live safe, healthy and fulfilling lives;
- responsible citizens who make a positive contribution to society.

Effective pedagogy (see also "Resources and pedagogic materials" in Chapter 2)

The Jump$tart framework does not include guidance about effective pedagogy. The other frameworks provide varying levels of guidance, from very limited guidance to extensive guidance that includes case studies of teaching practices and detailed lesson plans.

The recommended approaches to effective pedagogy include:

- opportunity to engage with "real-world" financial contexts;
- inquiry-based learning;
- critical engagement and discussion;
- problem-solving approaches involving student research and projects;
- cross-curricular approaches;
- activity-based approaches, including use of role-play and simulation.

The Japanese, New Zealand, English and Northern Ireland frameworks include case studies of teaching practices that demonstrate effective pedagogy. The Malaysian framework refers to sample lesson plans. The New Zealand and English frameworks provides guidance about the importance of creating a supportive learning environment in which students' cultural backgrounds and values are recognised.

The Malaysian framework refers to the ways Bank Negara Malaysia's financial education programme is being provided during the co-curriculum activities. The framework is also applicable for programmes designed for children with disabilities including those with learning disabilities.

The Scottish and the Dutch frameworks refer to opportunities provided by extra-curricular and community-based activities as contexts for developing financial literacy. The New Zealand, Malaysian and Dutch frameworks note the importance of involving families and communities in financial education programmes, as demonstrated by the text from the New Zealand framework below:

"Developing financial capability provides an authentic learning context to promote effective links between schools and other cultural contexts in which students grow up. There is opportunity for many productive partnerships to be formed with the community, including parents, whanau[2], agencies such as banks, budgeting advisers, and churches within the community."

Two school case studies are also provided to demonstrate these productive partnerships.

Assessment of students achievement

The English and Japanese frameworks provide specific guidance about assessment of student achievement. The English framework includes recommendations for day-to-day and periodic assessment in relation to the financial literacy outcomes and gathering evidence about the quality and effectiveness of the financial literacy programme across the school. The Japanese framework provides methods for assessing student achievement and case studies of effective teaching practice in the teaching resources also provide examples of ways to assess student achievement.

The Dutch framework illustrates how questions relating to financial education already come up in a number of established national tests (such as maths) and envisages for the future the importance of devising an appropriate evaluation programme in collaboration with the National Institute for Educational Measurement. In South Africa, assessment is conducted through the general procedures of the Ministry of Education, as stipulated on the Curriculum Assessment Policy Statements (2011).

None of the frameworks includes information about whether student achievement in financial education is assessed as part of national examinations.

The introduction of the Financial Literacy Option in the OECD Programme for International Students Assessment (PISA) in 2012 has also allowed the development of an assessment framework that can serve as a benchmark for policy makers and educational authorities worldwide (OECD, 2013) (see also "Evaluation of Financial Education Programmes", Chapter 2).

Teaching and learning resources (see also "Resources and pedagogic materials" in Chapter 2)

Most frameworks provide links to resources to support the teaching of financial education, most commonly in the form of web-based links. In some cases, the resources have not been developed specifically to support the implementation of the framework but are pre-existing resources that are considered relevant. Brazil is an exception in which teachers' books were especially developed for the pilot project. The Australian, English and Jump$tart frameworks provide guidance about selecting effective resources with the English 2008 and Jump$tart frameworks referring to specific quality assurance guidelines.

The Australian and English 2008 frameworks provide advice about working with external contributors from the finance and business communities and the importance of ensuring that there is no promotion of financial products or services. In Australia, teachers are also supported by a dedicated website (www.teaching.moneysmart.gov.au) which provides curriculum links, case studies and examples, divided by year level, learning area, audience and resource type, as well as links to state and territory financial literacy portals and a list of quality endorsed resources.

The South African framework recommends the use of textbooks and booklets developed by the FSBSA in co-ordination with the financial services sector and available in schools in print format with CD-Rom support. Financial institutions are deeply involved in the development of resources.

Professional development (see also "Training the teachers" in Chapter 2)

Frameworks can refer to professional development that is available to support teachers to incorporate financial education into their teaching. In Northern Ireland, free on-site workshops are provided in response to requests from schools and teachers. In Japan, the Central Council for Financial Services Information (CCFSI), the Local Councils for Financial Services Information, and the Japan Securities Dealers Association hold seminars and conferences to encourage teachers to introduce financial education. Most of the Jump$tart state coalitions offer teacher workshops to support financial education. In South Africa, the Department of Education is responsible for the professional development of teachers. The Financial Services Board also requires that all resources be mediated to teachers through special workshops.

The Australian Framework emphasises that professional learning is essential for the successful implementation of consumer and financial literacy. Australia in 2006 developed a nationally agreed professional learning strategy for teachers and in 2007 followed this up with a national professional learning package developed by the Australian Securities and Investments Commission (ASIC). The Australian Government provided national funding for professional learning which commenced in 2008 and is continuing as a priority.

Existing financial education learning frameworks

Financial education learning framework in Australia

History of the development of the framework

The Australian National Consumer and Financial Literacy Framework was first developed under the auspices of the then Ministerial Council for Education, Employment, Training and Youth Affairs in 2005 in response to a number of reports highlighting the need to improve Australian consumer and financial competencies. The approval of the National Framework through the Ministerial Council marked the starting point for national integration of consumer and financial literacy education in school curricula, with all ministers agreeing to make links with their state and territory curriculum frameworks in the compulsory years of schooling (Kindergarten – Year 10) from 2008.

With the growing international emphasis on financial education as a result of the global financial crisis and following the negotiation of new national goals for schooling in 2008[3], the National Framework's Rationale was updated in 2009. The advent of the national Australian Curriculum, which is being phased in over 2011–2016[4], prompted a second and more comprehensive review of the Framework in 2011[5] to ensure the dimensions and progression of student learning were better aligned with the new curriculum. These changes to the Framework were agreed by all education jurisdictions.

The development of a common Australian Curriculum provides an opportunity to achieve strengthened presence of consumer and financial literacy in schools and a measure of consistency in the curriculum links made. However states and territories will continue to have some flexibility in implementing the new Australian Curriculum.

Dimensions of financial education in the National Consumer and Financial Literacy Framework (2011)

There are three interrelated dimensions of learning that underpin consumer and financial education in the Australian context:

- Knowledge and Understanding;

- Competence; and,

- Responsibility and Enterprise

Knowledge and understanding

Students learn about the nature, forms and value of money; income and expenditure; and language commonly used in a range of consumer and financial contexts. They understand that money can come from a variety of sources and is used to meet and finance our needs and wants, now and in the future. Students develop a critical appreciation of the factors that affect consumer choices, including the impact of advertising, information communications technology (ICT) and media. They develop knowledge and understanding of consumer rights and responsibilities, the legal rights and responsibilities of business regarding goods and services provided to consumers, and the risks and complexities in the consumer and financial landscape. Students learn to identify scams and other risks and understand options for seeking advice or redress in consumer and financial contexts.

Competence

Students learn to appreciate that money is a finite resource and needs to be managed. In a variety of "real-life" contexts, they learn to use a range of practical tools and strategies (including IT, digital and online tools) to keep financial records, manage their finances on a daily basis, and to plan for the future. They understand the need to balance risk against reward and learn to work out "best value" when purchasing a range of goods and services and choosing financial products. They learn to discriminate between fact and opinion and to evaluate the claims made in advertising. Students also become alert to risks in a range of consumer and financial contexts and learn ways to manage these effectively.

Responsibility and enterprise

Students explore what it means to be a responsible and ethical consumer and learn how business has legal and ethical responsibilities towards consumers. They examine and reflect on their own roles as producers and consumers of goods and services and how this role fits into the broader national and global economic and social contexts. Students also explore the roles that socio-cultural influences and personal values play in consumer and financial decision-making and learn that there are often consequences of consumer and financial decisions that may impact not only on individuals, and their families but also on the broader community and the environment. Students exercise personal and shared responsibility and develop enterprising behaviours through the application of consumer and financial knowledge and skills in relevant class and/or school activities such as student investigations, charity fundraising, product design and development, business ventures and special events.

Learning outcomes

The framework provides "descriptions of learning" for each of the dimensions at four year levels. These are described in terms of learning outcomes. It is envisaged that the descriptions of learning in the National Consumer and Financial Literacy Framework will need to be revised in due course to accommodate links made with the new Australian Curriculum.

Year 2

Knowledge and understanding

Students can:

- recognise Australian money includes notes and coins;
- recognise that money is limited and comes from a variety of sources;
- recognise that money can be saved to meet needs and wants;
- explain how money is exchanged in return for goods and services;
- identify and describe the differences between needs and wants.

Competence

Students can:

- use money to buy basic goods and services in "real-life" contexts;
- recognise common symbols and terms used on a variety of Australian notes and coins;
- identify consumer and financial matters that are part of daily life such as earning money, spending, saving, paying bills, making donations;
- compare the cost of similar items;
- order spending preferences and explain reasons for their choices;
- describe how advertising can influence consumer choices.

Responsibility and enterprise

Students can:

- identify simple ways the consumer decisions of individuals may impact on themselves, their families, the broader community and/or the environment;
- identify and explain how peer pressure can affect what you buy;
- apply consumer and financial knowledge and skills in relevant class and/or school activities such as student investigations, charity fundraising, business ventures and special events;
- demonstrate enterprising behaviours through participation in relevant class and/or school activities;

- demonstrate awareness of safe, ethical and responsible behaviour in online and digital consumer and financial contexts;

- demonstrate awareness that family, community and socio-cultural values and customs can influence consumer behaviour and financial decision-making.

Year 4

Knowledge and understanding

Students can:

- explain some different forms that money can take;

- identify different forms of income;

- explain the role of work in society and distinguish between paid and unpaid work;

- explain how saving money in a financial institution can earn interest;

- explain why similar goods and services may vary in price;

- identify, explain and prioritise different needs and wants;

- recognise that different countries use different currencies.

Competence

Students can:

- use money to buy basic goods and services in "real-life" contexts;

- create simple budgets for specific purposes;

- accurately complete simple financial forms, including for online transactions;

- classify and compare goods and services;

- order and discuss reasons for spending preferences;

- discuss some options for paying for goods and services such as: cash, debit card, credit card and direct debit;

- identify key features of a range of advertisements.

Responsibility and enterprise

Students can:

- identify and describe the impact that the consumer and financial decisions of individuals may have on themselves and their families, the broader community and/or the environment;

- identify and explain how some influences, such as advertising and peer pressure, can affect what you buy;

- apply consumer and financial knowledge and skills in relevant class and/or school activities such as student investigations, charity fundraising, business ventures and special events;

- exercise a range of enterprising behaviours through participation in relevant class and/or school activities;

- describe safe, ethical and responsible behaviour in online and digital consumer and financial contexts;

- explain the role played by the voluntary sector in the community to help those in financial need;

- demonstrate awareness that family, community and socio-cultural values and customs can influence consumer behaviour and financial decision-making.

Year 6

Knowledge and understanding

Students can:

- explain how financial transactions can include using more than notes and coins;

- describe how an individual can influence their income;

- explore the value of unpaid work to the community;

- recognise that families use household income to meet regular financial commitments and immediate and future expenses;

- analyse the value of a range of goods and services in relation to an identified need;

- identify and discuss some rights and responsibilities of consumers and business;

- explain how money can be borrowed to meet needs and wants and that there may be a cost involved;

- recognise that the currencies of different countries have different values relative to the Australian dollar.

Competence

Students can:

- use a range of methods and tools to keep financial records in "real-life" contexts;

- create simple budgets for a range of purposes and explain the benefits of saving for future needs and wants;

- accurately complete and explain the purpose of financial forms, including for online transactions;

- evaluate the value of a range of goods and services in a variety of "real-life" situations;

- order and justify reasons for spending preferences;

- discuss various payment options for purchasing goods and services such as: cash, debit card, credit card, direct debit and PayPal;

- interpret information from a variety of invoice accounts including information presented graphically such as in electricity accounts;

- identify key features used in advertising, marketing and social media to influence consumer decision-making.

Responsibility and enterprise

Students can:

- identify and describe the impact that the consumer decisions of individuals may have on themselves and their families, the broader community and/or the environment;

- examine and discuss the external factors that influence consumer choices;

- explain there are ethical considerations to some consumer and financial decisions;

- apply consumer and financial knowledge and skills in relevant class and/or school activities such as student investigations, charity fundraising, product design and development, business ventures and special events;

- exercise a range of enterprising behaviours through participation in relevant class and/or school activities;

- practise safe, ethical and responsible behaviour in online and digital consumer and financial contexts;

- recognise that satisfaction derived from spending money varies according to the nature of the purchase, the context in which it is bought and an individual's personal circumstances and values;

- recognise that matching household expenditure against income is important;

- explain the role played by the voluntary sector in the community to help those in financial need;

- demonstrate awareness that family, community and socio-cultural values and customs can influence consumer behaviour and financial decision-making.

Year 8

Knowledge and understanding

Students can:

- identify and explain the importance of tracking and verifying transactions and keeping financial records to manage income and expenses;

- identify and discuss casual employment opportunities that can earn income;

- identify the role of casual employment in the community and some associated rights and responsibilities;

- explain why it is important to set and prioritise personal financial goals;

- research, identify and discuss the rights and responsibilities of consumers in a range of "real-life" contexts;

- research, identify and discuss the legal rights and responsibilities of business regarding goods and services provided to consumers;

- identify implications of "terms and conditions" such as fees, penalties, interest and warranties;

- identify and discuss the different forms of "credit" and costs involved;

- analyse and explain the range of factors affecting consumer choices;

- identify where to access reliable information and advice concerning the rights and responsibilities of consumers and business;

- identify the risks within the consumer and financial landscape such as scams, identity theft, fraudulent transactions and ways of avoiding these.

Competence

Students can:

- use a range of methods and tools to keep financial records in "real-life contexts";

- create simple budgets and financial records to achieve specific financial goals;

- compare income, spending commitments and life-styles at different stages of life;

- accurately complete and explain the purpose of a range of financial forms, including for online transactions;

- determine the value of "deals" when purchasing goods and services such as "buy one, get one free";

- determine and compare the actual cost of using different ways of paying for goods and services such as cash, credit, lay-by and loans;

- justify the selection of a range of goods and services in a variety of "real-life" contexts;

- convert from one currency to another in "real-life" contexts;

- explore the pros and cons of a range of payment options for goods and services such as: cash, debit card, credit card, direct debit, PayPal, BPay, pre-pay options, phone and electronic funds transfer;

- explain procedures for safe and secure online banking and shopping;

- identify and take precautions to prevent identity theft and explain what to do if this happens to them;

- access and evaluate information on strategies to resolve consumer disputes;

- identify and explain marketing strategies used in advertising and social media to influence consumer decision-making.

Responsibility and enterprise

Students can:

- explain how individual and collective consumer decisions may have an impact on the broader community and/or the environment;

- apply informed and assertive consumer decision-making in a range of "real-life" contexts;

- discuss the legal and ethical issues associated with advertising and providing goods and services to consumers;

- apply consumer and financial knowledge and skills in relevant class and/or school activities such as student investigations, charity fundraising, product design and development, business ventures and special events;

- exercise a range of enterprising behaviours through participation in relevant class and/or school activities;

- practise safe, ethical and responsible behaviour in online and digital consumer and financial contexts;

- recognise the importance of planning for their financial futures and appreciate that sacrificing current expenditure can bring long-term benefits;

- recognise that people have different ways of living and expectations according to their values and/ or financial situation;

- recognise that their ability to make informed decisions about personal finance and financial products is strengthened by finding and evaluating relevant information and accessing reliable advice;

- explain the role of banks and other deposit-taking institutions (such as building societies and credit unions) in providing financial products and services to individual consumers and business;

- explain the role played by governments and the voluntary sector in the community to help those in financial need and explore the cost benefit to the economy;

- demonstrate awareness that family, community and socio-cultural values and customs can influence consumer behaviour and financial decision-making.

Year 10

Knowledge and understanding

Students can:

- identify and explain strategies to manage personal finances;

- explain the different ways in which people are paid including wages, salaries, commissions, self-employment and government benefits;

- identify and explain common terminology and categories for deductions used on pay slips;

- explain the various factors that may impact on achieving personal financial goals;

- discuss why some goods and services are provided by Government for community benefit and how these are funded;

- explain how over-reliance on credit can impact on future choices;

- analyse and explain the range of factors affecting consumer choices;

- discuss and compare different sources of consumer and financial advice;

- identify types of consumer and financial risks to individuals, families and the broader community, and ways of managing them.

Competence

Students can:

- use a range of methods and tools to keep financial records in "real-life contexts";

- create simple budgets and financial records to achieve specific financial goals, now and in the future;

- investigate the financial decisions required at significant life-stage events;

- accurately complete and explain the purpose of a range of financial forms, including for online transactions;

- discuss the differences between "good" and "bad" debt, including manageability of debt and its long-term impact;

- analyse relevant information to make informed choices when purchasing goods and services and/ or to resolve consumer choices;

- compare overall "value" of a range of goods and services using IT tools and comparison websites as appropriate;

- convert from one currency to another in "real-life" contexts;

- evaluate the range of payment options for goods and services such as: cash, debit card, credit card, direct debit, PayPal, BPay, pre-pay options, phone and electronic funds transfer across a variety of "real-life" contexts;

- explain procedures for safe and secure online banking and shopping;

- identify and take precautions to prevent identity theft and explain what to do if this happens to them;

- explain the procedures for resolving consumer disputes relating to a range of goods and services;

- evaluate marketing claims, for example in advertising and in social media, to influence consumers to purchase a range of goods and services.

Responsibility and enterprise

Students can:

- research and identify the ethical and moral dimensions of consumer choices in specific circumstances and the consequences for themselves, their families, the broader community and/or the environment;

- explore the economic cost of individual and collective consumer decisions on the broader community and the environment;

- apply informed and assertive consumer decision-making in a range of "real-life" contexts;

- research and discuss the legal and ethical rights and responsibilities of business in advertising and providing goods and services to consumers;

- apply consumer and financial knowledge and skills in relevant class and/or school activities such as student investigations, charity fundraising, product design and development, business ventures and special events;

- exercise a range of enterprising behaviours through participation in relevant class and/or school activities;

- practise safe, ethical and responsible behaviour in online and digital consumer and financial contexts;

- appreciate that there is often no one right answer in making financial decisions because these depend on individual circumstances, preferences and values;

- understand and explain the legal responsibilities of taking on debt, including the consequences of not paying;

- explain how, as financially active citizens, they fit into the broader economy and society through:
  - generating income and paying taxes
  - saving
  - spending
  - donating
  - investing

- explain the role of banks and other deposit taking institutions (e.g. credit unions, building societies) in collecting deposits, pooling savings and lending them to individuals and business;

- explain the role played by governments and the voluntary sector in the community to help those in financial need and explore the cost benefit to the economy;

- demonstrate awareness that family and socio-cultural values and customs can influence consumer behaviour and financial decisions.

Financial education learning framework in England, United Kingdom

History of the development of the framework

In England the National Curriculum is set by the Department for Education (DfE). A revised National Curriculum was published in September 2013 and will be taught from September 2014.

The new curriculum for England, to be implemented as of September 2014, will require financial education to be taught in English secondary schools in Maths (through financial mathematics) and Citizenship (covering the functions and uses of money, the importance of personal budgeting, and managing risk, income and expenditure, credit and debt, insurance, savings and pensions, as well as a range of other financial products and services). The DfE also undertook a review of the non-statutory subject Personal Social, Economic and Health Education (PSHE), confirming that financial education would also remain a key component of this subject covering economic wellbeing and financial capability.

In primary schools, the new national curriculum will require some financial education to be covered in maths including understanding the value of different denominations of coins and notes and solving simple problems in a practical context involving money. The subjective side of financial education is taught in many primary schools through the non-statutory PSHE subject with the broad guideline that pupils should be taught to realise that money comes from different sources and can be used for different purposes.

Pfeg has produced a Secondary Planning Framework to support the teaching and assessment of financial education in the secondary phases of education across the United Kingdom in light of recent changes[6]. It is worth noting that this learning framework also takes into account the participation of England to the OECD Programme for International Student Assessment (PISA) Financial Literacy Option in 2015, and has been designed to cover all the areas of the PISA Financial Literacy Framework (OECD, 2013).

Even prior to the current revision of the Curriculum, the United Kingdom Government had set out its long-term aspiration to improve financial literacy in the United Kingdom including that every child has access to a planned and coherent programme of personal finance education in school. In July 2008, the Government and the Financial Services Authority (FSA) devised a joint action plan for financial literacy which included a significant programme of work to support personal financial education in schools.

This brought to the development of the 2008 English financial education framework, "Guidance on Financial Capability in the Curriculum: Key Stage 3 and 4", which was developed by the Department for Children, Schools and Families (DCSF, the predecessor of the DfE). It was a response to the push for the inclusion of financial education in schools by the Government and the FSA.

This framework, although not applicable anymore due to changes in the national curriculum, can be a good example to policy makers and education practitioners. The current revised national curriculum reflects the essential knowledge in key subjects that children should learn, giving teachers more autonomy to use their professional judgment to design curricula that meet the needs of their pupils.

The framework originally produced by DCSF in 2008 is provided below for reference.

Dimensions of financial education

- Knowledge and understanding: to inform young people's judgements and decisions about managing money in their present and future lives.

- Appropriate attitudes that are reflected in taking personal responsibility for money management, questioning the claims of some financial products and evaluating available information before making financial decisions.

- Financial skills that are demonstrated through day-to-day money management and planning for future financial needs, such as budgeting for weekly household items, monitoring bank accounts and credit cards and checking whether savings and investments are meeting financial goals.

Learning outcomes/standards

Learning outcomes are provided for each of the financial literacy concepts described above. Outcomes are expressed in terms of understanding, skills (what pupils will be able to do) and attitudes.

The following are the learning outcomes at key stage 3.

Pupils will understand:

- how wages/salaries are calculated;
- about different types of allowances and benefits available to me when I start independent life;
- different ways to pay goods and services and different forms of credit or debit arrangement;
- how holiday currency is arranged and how to calculate conversion rates;
- ways of choosing, opening and using different forms of bank account;
- how risk can be positive as well as negative and what basic financial decisions contain risks;
- how personal interest rates are calculated and how they vary according to the level of risk and length of commitment;
- the financial decisions are more about circumstances and personal choices than right answers;
- when typically insurance might be needed or not needed;
- how the stock market works, including positive and negative risks associated with it;
- the role of business in generating wealth- and what happens to it;
- how local services are paid for;
- the main forms of taxation;
- the role of charities and choices about giving to them;
- some effects of turbulence in the financial markets.

Pupils will be able to:

- estimate and calculate take-home pay for different occupations and circumstances;
- plan budgets for current weekly finances as a consumer;
- use different ways of recording spending and savings;
- choose financial products in different circumstances;
- find accurate information about choosing savings accounts and other financial products (minimising risk);
- consider the likelihood or otherwise of key national or international events affecting personal money;
- find and access advice about money.

Pupils will have explored attitudes to:

- priorities, needs, wants for the near future and later in life;

- how ineffective use of money can result in wasted resources;

- issues associated with gambling and how to avoid problems with it;

- environmental and ethical issues related to consumer choices.

The following are the learning outcomes at key stage 4.

Students will understand:

- how wages and salaries are calculated;

- how deductions such as tax, national insurance and pension contributes affect take home pay and what they are used for;

- implications of credit and debt (loans, overdrafts, mortgages), how costs accumulate over time;

- how insurance works and the types of insurance relevant to young people;

- how and why interest rates vary over time, according to the level of risk associated with them (including length of commitment) and how this can affect people;

- the differences between secured and unsecured loans and purchase agreements;

- the differences in risk and return between saving and investment products;

- the financial skills needed and risks involved in setting up and running a business;

- that private sector financial institutions make money through charging a higher rate of interest to borrowers than savers and by selling other financial services;

- how companies and other organisations are financed;

- how and why foreign exchange rates fluctuate;

- the main areas of national and local government finance and spending;

- rights and responsibilities re: financial products.

Students will be able to:

- identify financial qualities, attitudes and skills for employability;

- calculate young people's earnings and benefits including Education Maintenance Allowance and student finance/loans;

- compare the advantages and disadvantages of different forms of payment;

- balance income and expenditure – weekly and longer term budgeting;

- interpret bills and personal finance statements, extracting key information;

- calculate compound interest including the significance of AER (annual equivalent rate) and APR (annual percentage rate);

- find, use and evaluate financial advice and information from Internet, product advertising, financial advisors, Citizens Advice Bureau;

- use their knowledge of the market to work out the best deal in products and services;
- use understanding to calculate exchange rates;
- make basic risk/reward assessment in relation to saving and borrowing (and quantify the risk on the basis of past data);
- develop a sense of financial risk and recognise and learn from mistakes in financial decisions.

Students will have explored attitudes to:

- financial implications of career and other personal life choices/priorities;
- social, emotional and cultural factors influencing financial decisions;
- sacrificing current spending for long term benefits (e.g. investments, pensions, further and higher education);
- the risks and rewards related to gambling;
- local, national and global decisions that affect finances and impact on personal lives;
- personal spending in relation to fair trade, ethical trading, ethical investment.

Topics/issues covered and their goal

The framework does not provide a list of topics *per se*. However, PSHE education includes the majority of the curriculum's explicit financial literacy content, located in the economic wellbeing and financial literacy programmes of study. The key financial literacy concepts are:

Career:

- understanding that everyone has a "career" (and that this will affect personal finance).

Capability:

- exploring what it means to be enterprising;
- learning how to manage money and personal finances;
- becoming critical consumers of goods and services.

Risk:

- understanding risk in both positive and negative terms;
- understanding the need to manage risk in the context of financial and career choices;
- taking risks and learning from mistakes.

Economic understanding:

- understanding the economic and business environment;
- understanding the functions and use of money.

Range and content (topics)

- personal budgeting, wages, taxes, money management, credit, debt, and a range of financial products and services;

- risk and reward, and how money can make money through savings;

- investment and trade;

- how and why businesses use finance;

- social and moral dilemmas about the use of money.

The framework also includes guidance about the key processes to be used to teach financial literacy and the curriculum opportunities.

Key processes

Exploration:

- identify, select and use a range of information sources to research, clarify and review options and choices in career and financial contexts relevant to their needs.

Enterprise:

- assess, undertake and manage risk;

- demonstrate and apply understanding of economic ideas.

Financial literacy:

- manage their money;

- understand financial risk and reward;

- explain financial terms and products;

- identify how finance will play an important part in their lives and in achieving their aspirations.

Curriculum opportunities:

- use case studies, simulations, scenarios, role play and drama;

- have direct and indirect contact with people from business;

- engage with ideas, challenges and application from the business world;

- make links between economic wellbeing and financial literacy and other subjects and areas.

Financial education learning framework in Japan (see also Appendix 3.A2)

History of the development of the framework

The Central Council for Financial Services Information (CCFSI) has taken a leadership role in the development of a financial education framework for Japan. CCFSI is made up of representatives of associations of financial institutions and economic associations, associations of broadcasting companies, consumers' organisations and professors of education, consumer education and finance. CCFSI is funded by the Bank of Japan and other member organisations of CCSFI.

In 2006, the year in which the Basic Education Act of 1947 saw a full revision, CCFSI organised a committee involving scholars, senior officials from the Ministry of Education, Culture, Sports, Science and Technology, the National Institute of Educational Policies, the representatives of National Associations of School Principals to develop a financial education programme. The resulting document, "Financial Education Program - How to Cultivate the Ability to Live in the Society", was published by CCFSI in 2007.

In Japan, financial education in schools is taught as a cross-curricular subject in social studies, civic education and home economics.

Learning Outcomes

Topic: Financial life planning and household expenses management

Goals

Fund management skills and abilities of decision making:

- understanding that resources are limited;

- understanding the significance of building a better life under a limited budget and acquiring the attitude to practice it;

- understanding the basics of decisions making and acquiring the attitude to practice it.

Understanding the value of savings and the skill of asset management:

- understanding the significance of savings and acquiring the habit of saving;

- understanding the relationship between interest obtained and saving periods and recognising the importance of patience;

- understanding the risks and returns of various financial products and learning the attitude of investing under self-responsibility.

- Understanding the importance of life planning and obtaining skills for it:

- understanding the necessity of life planning and being able to make one's own life plan foreseeing the future;

- getting knowledge necessary for making one's own life plan;

- catching the future realistically relating it to life planning and occupational choice.

Topic: Mechanisms of the economy and financial system

Goals

- Understanding the functions of money and finance:

- understanding the roles and functions of money;

- understanding the roles of financial institutions and the functions of central banks;

- understanding the functions of interest rates.

- Understanding the mechanism of the economy:
- understanding the role of households, firms and governments and the circulation of goods and money;
- learning the functions of markets and understanding the significance of the market economy;
- understanding the relationship between industry development and the overseas economy.
- Understanding the fluctuations of the economy and the need for economic policy:
- understanding the relationship between business fluctuations, prices, interest rates, and stock prices;
- understanding the monetary policy of central banks and economic policy of the government;
- understanding how business fluctuations and economic policy are related to one's own life.
- Understanding various problems in the economy and the role of the government:
- getting interested in the wide-ranging problems that the economy is faced with;
- acquiring the attitude to think rationally and subjectively seeking for the settlement of a problem;
- understanding the role of the government.

Topic: Consumers' rights and risks and preventing financial trouble

Goals

- Obtaining basic skills to enable independent and appropriate decision making and to enable a fruitful life:
- becoming aware of rights and responsibilities of consumers;
- acquiring the attitude of acting as a self-reliant consumer;
- acquiring the skills of gathering of information and utilising it accurately.
- Prevent consumer troubles concerning financial transactions and multiple debt problems:
- learning the actual situation of financial troubles and multiple debt problems and acquiring the attitude needed to avoid them;
- learning the skills of dealing with troubles utilising laws and social systems.
- Becoming sensible consumers:
- understanding the meaning of controlling one's desire and acquiring the attitude to do so in one's daily life;
- acquiring the attitude to think about better ways to deal with money.

Topic: Career education

Goals

- Understanding the meaning of work and the choice of occupation:
- understanding the significance of work and the value of money;
- acquiring the attitude of thinking about one's occupational choice subjectively;
- understanding the rights and obligations of workers.
- Willingness to live and having vitality:
- understanding the various efforts are needed to produce added value;
- understanding that the creation of added value is the motive power for the development of the economy and society;
- acquiring the attitude to have a dream and to make efforts towards its realisation.
- Having gratitude for society and being willing to contribute to its improvement:
- understanding that people have various ties with society and cultivating the mind to keep rules and to have gratitude for others;
- cultivating the attitude of thinking about and practicing what one can do to improve society.

Financial education learning framework in Malaysia

History of the development of the framework

Bank Negara Malaysia, in collaboration with the Ministry of Education, has put forward a proposal (September 2013) for the introduction of financial education in the new 2014 school curriculum for primary schools and in 2017 for secondary schools. Under this proposal, financial education would be integrated into Bahasa Malaysia (as a stand-alone topic), Mathematics (as a stand-alone topic), English, Commerce and Economics.

The curriculum currently in place was developed in 2006 by the Bank, in collaboration with the Ministry of Education and financial institutions that participate in the Schools Adoption Programme (SAP), The framework is for the time being used as a guide for financial education programmes conducted during the co-curriculum activities.

The SAP was introduced in 1997 as a way of inculcating savings and smart money management habits among school children, with the emphasis shifting to financial education by 2001.

Learning outcomes

The framework provides learning outcomes for each of the three dimensions of financial education.

Financial knowledge and understanding

The children should be able to demonstrate their understanding on:

- the nature and role of money in society
- sources of income;
- spending, savings and investment;
- credit and debt;
- financial services/products and advisory services;
- consumer rights, responsibilities and protection;
- the impact of advertising, ICT (information and communications technology) on managing finances.

Financial skills and competence

The children should be able to:

- keep financial records;
- analyse financial information;
- assess value of money;
- prepare and use budgets;
- make informed financial decisions.

Financial responsibility

The children should be able to:

- take increasing responsibility for making decisions with respect to themselves;
- analyse the potential impact of financial decisions on their family and community;
- evaluate potential risk and returns.

Topics/issues covered and goals

Primary School Children (7 to 12 years of age)

1. Money / income

   - recognising and counting coins and notes of Malaysian currency;
   - currencies used in neighbouring countries;
   - sources of income (earned and unearned);
   - relationship between types of job and income earned.

2. Money management

   - money is a limited resource;

- managing money to fulfil one's future wants and needs;
- prioritising, i.e. differentiating between needs and wants;
- saving money and other resources (e.g. electricity).

3. Spending and debt

- simple planning and budgeting;
- borrowing money from friends is a bad habit;
- facts in advertisements can be misleading.

4. Savings and investment

- benefits of saving;
- how money grows through compounding;
- differences between savings and investment.

Secondary School Children (13 to 17 years of age)

1. Money / income

- various sources of income, e.g. return on investment, savings interest or rent;
- relationship between income, career choice and education requirement;
- inflation affects the purchasing power for goods and services.

2. Money management

- setting short- and medium-term financial goals;
- making a financial decision making process;
- designing a personal financial plan.

3. Spending and debt

- opportunity cost occurs in every spending decision;
- compare value of goods and services to get the best value for money;
- various payment methods that people pay for goods and services;
- benefits of costs of various types of consumer credit;
- calculation of how interest affects borrowing cost;
- describe rights and responsibilities of buyers and sellers under consumer protection laws

4. Savings and investment

- appropriate financial products for different financial goals such as bank accounts for savings and stocks for investment;
- compare the risk, return and liquidity of investment alternatives;

- various factors affect the rate of returns of investment;

- calculate amount of savings accumulated given different times, rates of return and frequencies of compounding;

- how money grows through compounding.

5. Risk management

- risk management strategies;

- insurance as a mean to transfer risk;

- types of insurance;

- how to recognise and avoid financial scam and identity theft.

Professional Development of Teachers

Bank Negara Malaysia in collaboration with the Ministry of Education and participating financial institutions in the School Adoption Programme conducts annual workshops to train teachers on how to deliver effective financial education activities. This is part of the professional development programmes for teachers.

Teachers' Learning Resources

Lesson plans are being used by teachers and financial institutions as a guide in conducting financial education activities. Lesson plans on financial education activities developed by teachers are based on learning outcomes and topics provided in the framework.

Financial education learning framework in the Netherlands (see also Appendix 3.A3)

History of the development of the framework

In 2006, some 40 partners from the financial sector, the government, the field of science, and public information and consumer organisations concluded an agreement to work towards financial education, entitled CentiQ, the Money-Wise Guide. Some partners to this agreement included the Ministry of Finance, the Ministry of Social Affairs and Employment, the Netherlands Authority for the Financial Markets (AFM), the General Pension Fund for Public Employees (ABP), Nibud (National Institute for Family Finance Information), the Fortis Foundation, the Consumers' Association, and the Netherlands Institute for Curriculum Development (SLO). A schedule of activities oriented towards a five-year implementation period (2009-2013) was drawn up in 2008 (CentiQ, 2008). In 2008 Dutch authorities began the implementation of the national strategy for financial education, the Money Wise Platform, under the leadership of the Ministry of Finance.

Nibud developed a first framework in 2008 (Nibud, 2009) setting out the competences and learning goals for children and adolescents when dealing with money. In 2012 Nibud decided to update the framework in order to reflect the new insights from research, the experience gained in its implementation, and to match more closely the competencies defined by the PISA Financial Literacy Framework (OECD, 2013).

These frameworks have informed all the financial education activities and related pedagogical materials developed within Dutch schools. The one developed in 2013 is currently being used as a reference in the talks with the Ministry of Economic Affairs for the development of a Financial Education and Entrepreneurship programme in Dutch schools, and is provided by the Ministry of Finance as a framework to publishers and authors drafting financial education materials and resources.

Competences and final goals

The "Nibud learning goals and competences" (Nibud, 2013) underline that learning to deal with money is becoming increasingly important for today's children and adolescents, and that it is pivotal to ensure a smooth transition to independence, to avoid financial problems as well as to ensure social participation. Nibud believes that learning how to deal with money should be among the main attainment goals in education, and as such establishes very specific links with some of the goals for key subjects of the Dutch curriculum (in Arithmetic and mathematics, People and society, Economics, Career and practical discovery, Learning career and citizenship).

The framework divides students in four age groups: lower primary school (6-8, higher primary school (9-11), lower intermediary school (12-14) and upper secondary school/intermediate vocational school (15-17). The description of learning goals indicates what children are capable of at a given age, but does not intend to set actual behaviours.

The framework identifies five themes: three themes identified as core competencies (mapping, responsible spending and anticipating) and two support competencies to the first three (dealing with financial risks, and having sufficient knowledge). The final goals, i.e. what adolescents should know by the time they are 18, for each theme are set out below. A detailed framework with learning goals by age and theme is provided in Annex 3.3.

Main theme 1: mapping

Adolescents are able to keep clear accounts so that they know where they stand and can find information easily. This allows them to meet payment obligations and understand how to keep their income and expenditure balanced.

Topics:

- Keeping proper accounts.
- Performing transactions.
- Earning money of your own.
- Keeping track of income and expenditure.

Main theme 2: responsible spending

Adolescents spend their income so that their income and expenditure are balanced in the short term. Their purchasing behaviour is in keeping with their personal preferences and what they can afford.

Topics:

- Making choices.

- Controlling temptation.
- Comparing prices and products.

Main theme 3: anticipating

Adolescents understand that wishes and events have medium- and long-term financial consequences and they take account of this, among other things by assessing opportunities to save and borrow money and obtain insurance.

Topics:

- Financial planning.
- Saving.
- Dealing with loans.
- Obtaining insurance.

Main them 4: dealing with financial risks

Adolescents are aware of the financial risks associated with situations, events and financial products. In the light of what they can afford, they make choices that take account of their personal situation and preferences and the associated risks.

Main topics:

- Assessing the financial consequences and risks of events and situations.
- Assessing the risks and yields of products with financial consequences.

Main theme 5: having sufficient knowledge (knowing the financial landscape)

Adolescents have all the relevant knowledge to balance their income and expenditure and keep them balanced in the short, medium and long term.

Topics:

- Knowing the value of money.
- Having knowledge of financial concepts and topics.
- Knowing their rights and duties as consumers and employees.
- Being able to obtain advice and help on money matters.

Financial education learning framework in New Zealand (see also Appendix 3.A4)

History of the development of the framework

Financial education in schools forms part of the National Strategy on Financial Literacy that the Commission for Financial Literacy and Retirement Income implements in New Zealand. A draft framework for financial education was developed by the Commission and responsibility for the promotion and development of financial education in schools was then transferred to the Ministry of Education in July 2009 and finalised[7].

Learning outcomes/standards

The framework initially developed by the Commission provided "possible progressions of learning"[8]. These are presented as learning outcomes for curriculum levels 1 to 5 across two strands:

1. Managing money and income

2. Setting goals and planning ahead

A revised and updated version of the progressions of learning is reproduced in Appendix 3.4.

Topics/issues covered and goals

Topics covered are referred to as "themes" for each of the two strands.

Managing money and income:

- Money.
- Income.
- Saving.
- Spending and budgeting.
- Credit.

Setting goals and planning ahead:

- Setting financial goals.
- Identifying and managing risk.

Financial education learning framework in Northern Ireland, United Kingdom

History of development

In 2007, the United Kingdom Government set out its long-term aspiration to improve financial literacy in the United Kingdom including that every child has access to a planned and coherent programme of personal finance education in school. In July 2008, the Government and the Financial Services Authority (FSA) set out a joint action plan for financial literacy which included a significant programme of work to support personal financial education in schools.

The Northern Ireland framework for financial education is provided on a dedicated website: "Northern Ireland Curriculum Financial Capability" developed in 2007[9]. The website is the responsibility of the Northern Ireland Executive, Council for the Curriculum, examinations and Assessment (CCEA).

Learning outcomes/standards

Learning outcomes are provided for each of the above dimensions.

1. Financial knowledge and understanding: Desired outcomes. Pupils will:

- develop the skills required to deal with everyday financial issues; and

- be able to make informed decisions and choices about personal finances.

2. Financial skills and competence: Desired outcomes. Pupils will:

    - be able to identify and tackle problems or issues with confidence; and

    - be able to manage financial situations effectively and efficiently.

3. Financial responsibility: Desired outcomes. Pupils will:

    - be aware that financial decisions and actions are closely linked with value judgements (social, moral, aesthetic, cultural and environmental as well as economic) and therefore have social and ethical dimensions.

Topics/issues covered and goals

The framework provides a statement of the topics/issues to be covered and their goals at each key stage. These are presented in two ways. The first is a description of what students will learn at each stage. These are as follows:

Foundation Stage: beginning to learn about and to manage their money.

During the Foundation Stage, children talk about the need to pay for goods (the exchange of goods for money). They learn about the different payment methods (cash, cheque, credit/debit card). They talk about and recognise coins (from 1p to £2) in various contexts and role-play activities, becoming familiar with coins in everyday use. They talk about where money comes from, how to get it and how to keep it safe. Children explore what to spend their money on and how it makes them feel. They talk about what it means to have more than needed and what can be done with extra money.

Key Stage 1: laying financial foundations for the future.

During Key Stage 1, children learn about money and making real choices about spending and saving money in the context of their own lives, including how to solve whole number problems involving money. They learn that money comes from different sources and can be used for different purposes. They learn about the importance of looking after money and that people will make different choices when spending their money. They learn about social and moral issues about the use of money in everyday lives.

Key Stage 2: learning to manage money and spend wisely.

During Key Stage 2, pupils learn about making simple financial decisions and consider how to spend their money e.g. pocket money and contributions to charity. They learn that their decisions can have individual, social and environmental consequences. They explore the concepts of earnings, expenses and budgeting. By learning how to look after money, they begin to understand that financial circumstances and standards of living can vary across time and place. They explore the different values and attitudes that people have with regard to money.

Key Stage 3: what influences you when it comes to spending money?

At this stage, pupils need to learn about what influences how we spend or save money and how to become competent at managing personal money in a range of situations including those beyond their immediate experience. They learn how local and central government is financed. They learn about insurance and risk and about making safer choices about healthy lifestyles. They learn about social and moral dilemmas and about the use of money including how the choices they make as consumers affect other people's economies and environments. They learn to solve complex numerical problems involving money including calculating percentages, ratio and proportion.

Key Stage 4: learn about the importance of managing money.

During Key Stage 4, pupils learn about financial decision-making and money management and to use a range of financial tools and services, including budgeting and saving, in managing personal money. They learn about, and how to assess the different sources of financial help and advice available to them. They learn about how the economy functions and the rights and responsibilities of consumers, employers and employees. They learn about the different risks and returns involved in savings and investments. They develop an understanding of the wider social, moral, ethical and environmental consequences of personal financial decisions. They continue to learn to solve complex numerical problems involving money including calculating percentages, ratios and proportions.

Detailed overviews of financial literacy in the curriculum are provided for each Key Stage. These include a list of topics to be covered for each of the dimensions. As an example, in Foundation Stage and Key Stage 1 these are:

Financial knowledge and understanding:

- what money is and the exchange of money.
- where money comes from.
- where money goes.

Financial competence:

- looking after money.
- spending money and budgeting.
- financial records and information.
- risk and return.

Financial responsibility:

- making personal life choices.
- consumer rights and responsibilities.
- the implications of finance.

Financial education learning framework in Scotland, United Kingdom

History of the development of the framework

In July 1998, the Scottish Consultative Council on the Curriculum (CCC) embarked on a project, supported by the Royal Bank of Scotland, to examine ways of developing education for financial literacy in schools. The project had two tasks: to develop a framework to aid thinking about financial education in schools; and to develop guidance and support materials for school managers and teachers to assist them with the development of financial education in schools.

"Financial Education in Scottish Schools A Statement of Position" (1999)[10] was the end-product of the first task described above. It was based on a discussion paper prepared during 1988 by an advisory group with a remit from Scottish CCC to produce a succinct and coherent statement on personal financial education. The outcome of the group's work was endorsed by the Council as a basis for consultation and published as a consultation document. The Council's statement of position was essentially a re-statement of the advisory group's ideas.

Since then, financial education has become a cross-cutting theme within the Scottish Curriculum, which all schools need to address. Financial education is one of the components of a lifelong learning strategy adopted in Scotland to ensure that every young person develops the knowledge and skills they will need for life, learning and work.

The Scottish Government, in partnership with Education Scotland and the Scottish Qualifications Authority (SQA) have developed the "Curriculum for Excellence"[11], which aims to support learners in the development of these skills. Education Scotland recognises the importance of financial literacy for all young people (Learning Teaching Scotland, 2010). They have identified four relevant aspects of financial capability: financial understanding, financial competence, financial responsibility and financial enterprise and these have been woven into Numeracy across Learning. This programme was developed from 2002, implemented in 2010 and will continue until 2016 when new qualifications, currently being developed by SQA, will be introduced.

Learning outcomes/standards

Learning outcomes are given for each dimension of financial literacy. The learning outcomes are a statement of what young people should be able to do. The learning outcomes are not assigned to particular key stages.

Learning outcomes related to financial understanding

As a result of learning experiences, young people should be able to demonstrate an understanding and critical appreciation of:

- the nature and role of money in society, including foreign currency;
- sources of income;
- taxation, spending, saving and investment, credit and debt;
- financial services/products and advisory services;
- consumer rights, responsibilities and protection;
- the impact of advertising, ICT and the media.

Learning outcomes related to financial competence

As a result of learning experiences, young people should be able to:

- keep financial records;
- analyse financial information;
- assess value for money;

- prepare and use budgets;
- make informed financial decisions.

Learning outcomes related to financial responsibility.

As a result of learning experiences, young people should be able to:

- take increasing responsibility for making decisions with respect to themselves;
- analyse the potential impact of financial decisions made by others on society and the environment both locally and globally;
- analyse the potential impact of their financial decisions on other people and the environment both locally and globally.

Learning outcomes related to financial enterprise.

As a result of learning experiences, young people should be able to:

- evaluate potential risks and returns;
- use financial and other resources in an innovative and confident manner;
- apply knowledge and skills creatively in a range of situations.

Topics/issues covered and their goal

The framework does not provide a list of topics/issues to be covered. The approach is to describe the intended learning outcome for financial literacy and then to describe the opportunities that exist within the existing curriculum from 5 to 18 to integrate financial literacy.

Examples of opportunities for financial learning in specific subjects are provided, but these are fairly non-specific and can't be reduced to a list of topics.

Financial education learning framework in South Africa

History and development of the framework

The South African Government, through its Department of Basic Education (DBE) has opted to integrate financial literacy into learning areas and subjects within the National Curriculum Statement (NCS) Curriculum Assessment and Policy Statements (CAPS) of South Africa. The NCS CAPS structures the curriculum into learning areas and subjects, grade level and amount of content to be covered in each academic year in South Africa. There is no single framework for financial literacy, but financial literacy is mentioned within the topic areas of learning outcomes of specific subjects. The learning areas and subjects into which financial literacy is integrated are Economic and Management Sciences, Accounting, Business and Economic Sciences, Mathematical Literacy and Consumer Studies.

The Financial Services Board (FSBSA) has a Consumer Education strategy which includes two programmes. These are Community Education and Formal Education. The Formal Education programme aims to promote the integration of financial consumer education into the formal education curriculum. This is done in consultation with the DBE and provincial education departments.

Framework goals

The financial literacy goals of the above mentioned subjects are reflected in their weightings within the curriculum and the topic covered. These are:

Economic and Management Sciences (grade 7-9)

Weighting within the curriculum	Topic
The economy (Weighting of 30%)	1. History of money 2. Need and wants 3. Goods and services 4. Inequality and poverty 5. The production process 6. Government 7. The National Budget 8. Standard of living 9. Markets 10. Economic systems 11. The circular flow 12. Price theory 13. Trade unions
Financial literacy (Weighting of 40%)	1. Savings 2. Budgets 3. Income and expenditure 4. Accounting concepts 5. Accounting cycle 6. Source documents 7. Financial management and keeping of records
Entrepreneurship (Weighting of 30%)	1. Entrepreneurial skills and knowledge 2. Businesses 3. Factors of production 4. Forms of ownership 5. Sectors of the economy 6. Levels and functions of management 7. Functions of a business 8. Business plan

Mathematical Literacy (Grade 10-12)

Weighting within the curriculum	Topic
Finance (Weighting of 35%)	1. Financial documents 2. Tariff systems 3. Income, expenditure, profit/loss, 4. income-and-expenditure statements and budgets 5. Cost price and selling price 6. Break-even analysis 7. Interest 8. Banking, loans and investments banking 9. Inflation 10. Taxation 11. Exchange rates

Accounting (Grade 10-12)

Weighting of curriculum	Topic
Financial Accounting (weighting 50% to 60%)	1. Accounting concepts 2. GAAP principles 3. Bookkeeping 4. Accounting equation 5. Final accounts and financial statements 6. Salaries and wages 7. Value-Added Tax 8. Reconciliations
Managerial Accounting (weighting 20% to 25%)	1. Cost accounting 2. Budgeting
Managing Resources (weighting 20% to 25%)	1. Indigenous bookkeeping systems 2. Fixed assets 3. Inventory 4. Ethics 5. Internal control

Endorsement

The South African National Curriculum Statement (NCS), which includes all learning areas and subjects mentioned, was first partially introduced in 1998 as "Curriculum 2005". It was revised in 2000 and fully introduced as the NCS in 2004. In 2010 the DBE undertook a review the NCS and the amended NCS and CAPS was phased into schools from 2012 and will complete in 2014. The FSBSA started implementing its consumer education strategy in 2002.

There is no specific body responsible for promoting financial education in schools. The FSBSA has attempted to play a coordinating role by engaging with industry bodies. Most institutions in the financial sector, however, implement their own financial education programmes, which leads to duplication in many instances. It is envisioned with the formulation of the National Consumer Financial Education Committee in 2011 that these efforts will become more structured thus largely eliminating duplications.

Assessment

Evaluation of learning takes place through the normal assessment strategies of the Department of Basic Education, as stipulated in the NCS subjects. Assessment is thus not on financial literacy, but rather in the achievement of the learning outcomes of each learning area and subject.

Topics/issues covered

The following shows the amount of financial education per subject and learning area:

- Economic and Management Sciences – up to 100%.

- Mathematical Literacy – 35 %.

- Accounting – 25 %.

- Business and Economic sciences – 20 %.

- Consumer Studies – 10 %.

Thus, while financial literacy is not taught as a stand-alone subject or learning area, it is integrated into the daily curriculum and not as an add-on that could be discontinued at any time for financial or other reasons.

The FSBSA's financial education is based on the following topics:

- Debt management.
- Savings.
- Budgeting.
- Credit.
- Caution against scams.
- Insurance.
- Retirement.
- Investments.
- Recourse.
- Rights and responsibilities.

Levels covered

All grades in schools (1-12).

Effective pedagogy

The NCS is delivered through an Outcome-based Education methodology, an approach that focuses on identifying desired outcomes and measuring success against these.

Teaching and learning resources

Teachers use textbooks and resources as prescribed by the education department for curriculum delivery. Alongside this, the FSBSA has attempted to provide a common framework by working with the Financial Services Sector to develop three booklets that provide the basis for financial consumer education. Themes therein include:

- Debt Management.
- Budgeting.
- Saving.
- Financial Risks.
- Insurance.
- Recourse.
- Rights and Responsibilities of consumers.

The resource materials are mostly in print format with CD-ROM support for schools with an ICT infrastructure. Each financial institution that provides financial literacy in schools, develops their own resources. The resources include:

- Three booklets, namely: Make the Most of Your Money, Use Your Money Wisely and Make Your Money Work for You. These booklets range from being very graphic to more textual in the third one to accommodate literacy levels.

- Managing Your Money – A booklet and two posters for teachers of Grade 10, 11 and 12 Mathematical literacy.

- Money in Action – a booklet and accompanying poster which covers grade 7-9 in South Africa.

Professional development

The Department of Basic Education is responsible for the professional development of teachers and this is done internally on a regular basis. The FSBSA makes all its resources available to teachers through workshops that demonstrate how to effectively use the resources in the classroom.

Financial education learning framework in the United States (Jump$tart)

History of the development of the framework

The Jump$tart Coalition issued its first Personal Finance Guidelines and Benchmarks in 1998, developed by a broad range of education, government and financial services organisations. The national standards were subsequently revised, updated in 2001 and 2006 and also reviewed by a group of finance and business industry professionals and educators in the third edition in 2007, National Standards in K-12 Personal Financial Education[12].

The Jump$tart Coalition for Personal Financial Literacy is a not-for-profit organisation that consists of 180 business, financial and educational organisations and 47 affiliated state coalitions dedicated to improving the financial literacy of youth.

Learning outcomes/standards

The national standards provide "knowledge statements" of the "overall competency" that students are expected to develop for each of the dimensions of personal finance. As well as the overall competency statement, more detailed descriptions are provided of the knowledge that students at 4th Grade, 8th Grade and 12th Grade are expected to be able to exhibit.

The overall competency statements are as follows:

- financial responsibility and decision making: apply reliable information and systematic decision making to personal financial decisions;

- income and careers: use a career plan to develop personal income potential;

- planning and money management: organise personal finances and use a budget to manage cash flow;

- credit and debt: maintain credit worthiness, borrow at favourable terms, and manage debt;

- risk management and insurance: use appropriate and cost-effective risk management strategies;

- saving and investment: implement a diversified investment strategy that is compatible with personal goals.

Topics/issues covered and their goals

Broad topics/issues are provided in the form of standards for each of the dimensions of personal finance education. These are in the form of overall standards which are expanded into expectations for each of the standards at 4th grade, 8th grade and 12th grade. The following are the overall standards for each of the dimensions:

Financial responsibility and decision making:

Standard 1: take responsibility for personal financial decisions.
Standard 2: find and evaluate financial information from a variety of sources.
Standard 3: summarise major consumer protection laws.
Standard 4: make financial decisions by systematically considering alternatives and consequences.
Standard 5: develop communication strategies for discussing financial issues.
Standard 6: control personal information.

Income and careers

Standard 1: explore career options.
Standard 2: identify sources of personal income.
Standard 3: describe factors affecting take-home pay.

Planning and money management

Standard 1: develop a plan for spending and saving.
Standard 2: develop a system for keeping and using financial records.
Standard 3: describe how to use different payment methods.
Standard 4: apply consumer skills to purchase decisions.
Standard 5: consider charitable giving.
Standard 6: develop a personal financial plan.
Standard 7: examine the purpose and importance of a will.

Credit and debt

Standard 1: identify the costs and benefits of various types of credit.
Standard 2: explain the purpose of a credit record and identify borrowers' credit report rights.
Standard 3: describe ways to avoid or correct debt problems.
Standard 4: summarise major consumer credit laws.

Risk management and insurance

Standard 1: identify common types of risk and basic risk management methods.
Standard 2: explain the purpose and importance of property and liability protection insurance.
Standard 3: explain the purpose and importance of health, disability, and life insurance protection.

Saving and investing

Standard 1: discuss how saving contributes to financial well-being.
Standard 2: explain how investing builds wealth and helps meet financial goals.
Standard 3: evaluate investment alternatives.
Standard 4: describe how to buy and sell investments.
Standard 5: explain how taxes affect the rate of return on investments.
Standard 6: investigate how agencies that regulate financial markets protect investors.

Notes

1. Australian Ministerial Council on Education, Employment, Training and Youth Affairs (2011).

2. Māori language word for extended family

3. http://www.mceecdya.edu.au/mceecdya/national_goals_for_schooling_working_group,24776.html

4. See http://www.acara.edu.au/curriculum/curriculum.html

5. Available at http://www.mceecdya.edu.au/verve/_resources/National_Consumer_Financial_Literacy_Framework_FINAL.pdf

6. More information is available at http://www.pfeg.org/resources/details/secondary-planning-framework-framework-11-16-yrs

7. Additional information can be found at www.nzcurriculum.tki.org.nz/

8. Ministry of Education of New Zealand (2009).

9. www.nicurriculum.org.uk/microsite/financial_capability/

10. Learning Teaching Scotland (1999).

11. More information is available at: http://www.educationscotland.gov.uk/thecurriculum/whatiscurriculumforexcellence/keydocs/index.asp

12. Jump$tart Coalition for Personal Financial Literacy (2007).

References

OECD Recommendations

OECD (2005), Recommendation on Principles and Good Practices on Financial Education and Awareness, http://www.oecd.org/finance/financial-education/35108560.pdf

OECD/INFE instruments and relevant outputs

INFE (2010a), Guide to Evaluating Financial Education Programmes, available at *www.financial-education.org.*

INFE (2010b), Detailed Guide to Evaluating Financial Education Programmes, available at *www.financial-education.org.*

INFE (2011), High-level Principles for the Evaluation of Financial Education Programmes, available at *www.financial-education.org.*

OECD (2004), "ISCED Mappings of Countries' National Programmes to ISCED Levels", in OECD, *OECD Handbook for Internationally Comparative Education Statistics: Concepts, Standards, Definitions and Classifications,* OECD Publishing. doi: 10.1787/9789264104112-8-en

OECD (2013), "Financial Literacy Framework", in OECD, PISA 2012 Assessment and Analytical Framework: Mathematics, Reading, Science, Problem Solving and Financial Literacy, OECD Publishing. doi: 10.1787/9789264190511-7-en

Other

Australian Ministerial Council on Education, Employment, Training and Youth Affairs (2011), National Consumer and Financial Literacy Framework available at *www.mceecdya.edu.au/verve/_resources/National_Consumer_Financial_Literacy_Fr amework_FINAL.pdf*

COREMEC, Comitê de Regulação e Fiscalização dos Mercados Financeiro, de Capitais, de Seguros, de Previdência e Capitalização (2009), "Orientação para Educação Financeira nas Escolas", *Estratégia Nacional de Educação Financeira – Anexos,* available at *www.vidaedinheiro.gov.br/Imagens/Plano%20Diretor%20ENEF%20-%20anexos.pdf*

Department for Children, Schools and Families (2008), Guidance on Financial Capability in the Curriculum: Key Stage 3 and 4, available at *https://www.education.gov.uk/publications/standard/Educationstages/Page1/DCSF-00645-2008*

European Commission, Eurydice - Eurypedia The European Encyclopedia on National Education Systems, *https://webgate.ec.europa.eu/fpfis/mwikis/eurydice/index.php?title=Home*

Jump$tart Coalition for Personal Financial Literacy (2007), National Standards in K–12 Personal Finance Education with Benchmarks, Knowledge Statements, and Glossary, available at *www.jumpstart.org/assets/files/standard_book-ALL.pdf*

Learning Teaching Scotland (1999), Financial Education in Scottish Schools: A Statement of Position, available at *www.ltscotland.org.uk/Images/financialedstatement_tcm4-121478.pdf*

Learning Teaching Scotland (2010), Financial Education: Developing Skills for Learning, Life and Work, available at *http://www.educationscotland.gov.uk/Images/developing_skills_web_tcm4-639212.pdf*

Ministry of Education of New Zealand (2009), Financial Capability: Possible Progressions of Learning available at *http://nzcurriculum.tki.org.nz/Curriculum-resources/Learning-and-teaching-resources/Financial-capability/FC-progressions#ahead*

Nibud (2009), Learning to Manage Money - learning goals and competences for children and young people, available at *www.nibud.nl/fileadmin/user_upload/Documenten/PDF/nibud_learning_goals_and_competen ces.pdf*

Nibud (2013), Nibud Learning Goals and Competences for Children and Adolescents, available at http://www.nibud.nl/fileadmin/user_upload/Documenten/PDF/2013/Learning_goals_and_com petences_for_children_and_adolescents_eng_version_2013.pdf

OECD (2013), "Financial Literacy Framework", in OECD, *PISA 2012 Assessment and Analytical Framework: Mathematics, Reading, Science, Problem Solving and Financial Literacy*, OECD Publishing. doi: 10.1787/9789264190511-7-en

Appendix 3.A1

Comparison of financial education learning frameworks in selected countries

Table 3.A1.1. **Main characteristics of the frameworks**

	Endorsement by Government	Learning outcomes/ standards	Levels / age	Compulsory / statutory?
Australia	Yes	Yes	Kindergarten to Year 10	Largely not compulsory. However, a core sub-strand of the Australian Curriculum: Mathematics is "Money and financial mathematics" and there are plans for the new Economics and Business Curriculum to be mandatory in years 5-8.
Brazil	Yes	Yes	Secondary level (for the pilot exercise)	Not compulsory : implementation only as a pilot exercise in selected schools around the country
England, United Kingdom (2008)	Yes	Yes	Secondary level	Not compulsory
Japan	Yes	Yes	Across compulsory school sector to high school level	Not compulsory
Malaysia	Yes	Yes, but not levelled	Across compulsory school sector	Compulsory
The Netherlands	Yes	Yes	1-18	Not compulsory
New Zealand	Yes	Yes	Across all years of primary and secondary schooling, years 1-13	Not compulsory
Northern Ireland	Yes	Yes	Kindergarten to Year 10	Compulsory
Scotland, United Kingdom	Yes	Yes, but not levelled	Secondary level	As of 2008, financial education is a cross-cutting theme that all schools need to address
South Africa	Yes	Yes	7-12	Not compulsory
United States – Jump$tart	No- but subject to ongoing review	Yes	Across compulsory school sector	Not compulsory

Table 3.A1.2. Modalities of integration, assessment of outcomes and teaching practices

	Integrated or stand-alone subject?	Curriculum links	Effective pedagogy	Assessment and monitoring	Teaching and learning resources	Professional development
Australia	Integrated. Links to the Australian Curriculum	No specific guidance on teaching strategies. However the Framework underpins the content of the MoneySmart Teaching Programme.	Not included in the Framework *per se*, but in MoneySmart teaching resources.	Australian Council of Education Research to conduct an evaluation of the teaching of the MoneySmart programme pilot phase (2012).	Not specifically included in the framework but available through http://teaching.money smart.gov.au/	Yes http://teaching.money smart.gov.au/
Brazil	Integrated	NA	Yes including case study and real life content ; activities	Yes – full-fledged impact assessment	Yes - book provided	Yes
England, United Kingdom (2008)	Explicitly included in PSHE. Integrated in other subjects	Yes. PSHE, mathematics, citizenship and other subjects where relevant	Yes. Includes case studies	Yes	Yes – links provided	Yes
Japan	Integrated	Yes. Social studies; home economics; integrated studies; moral education; Japanese language; arithmetic	Yes. Includes case studies	Yes	Yes- resources provided	Yes
Malaysia	Integrated	Mainly mathematics, living skills, economics, commerce and other relevant subjects.	Yes	Not included	Yes – links provided	Yes. Relevant teachers are selected to attend the financial education annual workshops conducted by Bank Negara

	Integrated or stand-alone subject?	Curriculum links	Effective pedagogy	Assessment and monitoring	Teaching and learning resources	Professional development
						Malaysia in collaboration with the Ministry of Education and participating financial institutions under the School Adoption Programme.
Netherlands	Integrated	Yes. Provides a starting point	Yes	Yes	Yes	In a plan
New Zealand	Integrated and cross-curricular	Yes. Literacy and numeracy and other subjects where relevant	Yes. Includes case studies	Not included	Yes – links provided	Yes
Northern Ireland	Integrated	Yes. Mathematics and numeracy; personal development and mutual understanding; learning for life and work; the arts, English and Irish; modern languages; environment and society; science and technology	Yes. Includes case studies	Not included	Yes – links provided	Yes
South Africa	Integrated and cross-curricular	Yes. Economics and Management Sciences; Mathematics literacy;	Yes	Yes-normal DoE processes and procedures	Yes – links provided	Yes

	Integrated or stand-alone subject?	Curriculum links	Effective pedagogy	Assessment and monitoring	Teaching and learning resources	Professional development
		Accounting; Business and Economic sciences; Consumer Studies				
Scotland	Integrated	Yes. Personal and social development; mathematics, English; environmental studies; society, science and technology; modern languages; geography; modern studies; social and vocational skills; business management; craft and design; home economics	Yes	Not included	Not included in the framework but subsequently made available	Not included in the framework but subsequently made available
United States	Integrated or stand-alone depending on local needs	No- to be determined at the local level	Not included	Not included	Yes – links provided	Yes

Table 3.A1.3. Focus of the learning framework

	Focus	Definition or description
Australia	Consumer and financial literacy	"Individuals who are consumer and financially literate have the ability to apply knowledge, understanding, skills and values in consumer and financial contexts to make informed and effective decisions that have a positive impact on themselves, their families, the broader community and the environment."
Brazil	Financial literacy	Includes financial knowledge, understanding, skills and behaviours as well as social awareness
England, United Kingdom (2008)	Financial capability	"Financial capability is the ability to manage one's finances and to become a confident, questioning and informed consumer of financial services."
Japan	Financial education/pecuniary education	Financial education is defined as "an education that enables students to understand the function of money and finance, to deepen student's thoughts on their daily life, to improve their lifestyle and their sense of values, and to nurture voluntary attitudes towards improvement of their life and society."
Malaysia	Financial literacy	Financial literacy is defined as "a person's ability to make informed judgements, take effective decisions regarding the use and management of money, keep track of finances, planning ahead, choosing financial products, and staying informed about financial matters."
Netherlands	Financial capability	Strengthen consumers' position in the financial domain; "Financial Capability includes financial knowledge and understanding; financial skills and competences; financial responsibility."
New Zealand	Financial capability	"A financially capable person is able to make informed judgements and effective decisions regarding the personal use and management of money."
Northern Ireland	Financial capability	"Financial Capability is more that the ability to recognise coins or calculations involving money. It is an essential life skill which enhances their ability to make effective choices and become more financially responsible."
Scotland	Financial capability	"Financial capability involves knowing how to manage personal finances in the midst of a changing context of wider economic forces that affect people's lives and society as a whole. Becoming financially capable involves acquiring understanding, developing skills and fostering values. However, financial capability is about more than this. It means being able both to think critically about financial issues and to draw together and apply knowledge and skills in particular situations whilst having due regard to the

	Focus	Definition or description
		impact of financial decisions on people's lives and on the environment."
South Africa	Financial literacy	Financial literacy aims to enable people understand economic cycle, sustainable growth develop entrepreneurial knowledge; solve problems; understand financial information.
United States – Jump$tart	Personal finance and financial literacy	"Financial capability involves knowing how to manage personal finances in the midst of a changing context of wider economic forces that affect people's lives and society as a whole. Becoming financially capable involves acquiring understanding, developing skills and fostering values. However, financial capability is about more than this. It means being able both to think critically about financial issues and to draw together and apply knowledge and skills in particular situations whilst having due regard to the impact of financial decisions on people's lives and on the environment."

Table 3.A1.4. Dimensions included in financial education frameworks

	Knowledge and understanding	Skills and competencies/capability	Attitudes and values	Enterprise
Australia	✓	✓	✓	✓
Brazil	✓	✓	✓	
England, UK (2008)	✓	✓	✓	
Japan	✓	✓	✓	✓
Malaysia	✓	✓	✓	
Netherlands	✓	✓	✓	✓
New Zealand	✓	✓	✓	
Northern Ireland	✓	✓	✓	
Scotland	✓	✓	✓	✓
South Africa	✓	✓	✓	✓
United States – Jump$tart	✓	✓	✓	

Appendix 3.A2

Japan: Contents of financial education by age group[*]

[*] Source: Central Council for Financial Services Information "Financial Education Program", 2007, http://www.shiruporuto.jp/e/consumer/pdf/financial_education.pdf

Table 3.A2.1. Learning framework goals for different age groups

	Goals	Primary School Students			Secondary School Students	High School Students
		1st and 2nd grades	3rd and 4th grades	5th and 6th grades		
Financial life planning and household expenses management						
Budgeting	• Understanding that resources are limited (i.e. budgets are constrained). Understanding the significance of building a better life under a limited budget and acquiring the attitude to practice it. • Understanding the basics of decision making and acquiring the attitude to practice it.	• Learning the value of money and making much of goods and money. • Being able to buy goods within their budget.	• Recognising the difference between needs and wants. • Understanding scarcity of resources. • Being able to manage suitable amount of money for one's age.	• Being able to buy things according to their plan, taking indispensability into account. • Learning how to choose goods, and being able to contrive to buy goods. • Obtaining the attitude of making a decision based on one's own idea while understanding friends' idea.	• Deepening the understanding of household's income and expenditure. • Being able to choose, purchase and use necessary goods and services adequately. • Managing an expenditure and income practically (ex. Doing so for a school excursion). • Understanding the variety of people's senses of value through knowing how they use money.	• Understanding the importance of long run money management. • Making a balance practically (doing so for school events, etc.). • Understanding the importance of decision making through selecting one's career.
Saving, investing and use of financial	• Understanding the significance of savings and acquiring the habit	• Trying to save pocket money and a New Year's	• Understanding the significance of savings and	• Learning to plan to save thinking about what to spend in the	• Understanding stocks and bonds. • Thinking about the	• Understanding the characteristics of various

Goals	Primary School Students			Secondary School Students	High School Students
	1st and 2nd grades	3rd and 4th grades	5th and 6th grades		
products • Understanding the relationship between interests obtained and saving periods and recognising the importance of patience. • Understanding the risks and returns of various financial products and learning the attitude of investing under self responsibility.	present of money.	acquiring the habit of planning to save. • Obtaining the patience to complete tasks.	future. • Learning principal types of bank accounts and understanding the difference of interest rates on various kinds of deposits. • Being able to calculate simple interest rate.	meaning of investing money. • Understanding the relationship between risks and returns. • Learning the relationship between interests obtained (at compound interest) and the saving periods and obtaining the attitude to save money continuously.	financial products such as bank accounts, stocks, bonds, and insurances, etc.. • Understanding the risks and returns of financial products. • Being conscious of making decision self-responsibly taking portfolio balance into account. • Thinking about the difference between investment and speculation.
Understanding the importance of life planning • Understanding the necessity of life planning and being able to make one's own	• Becoming aware of the necessity of planning	• Recording the pocket money account.	• Understanding the importance of using money according to	• Understanding the necessity of life planning and making a life plan	• Making a life plan and grasping one's lifetime income

	Goals	Primary School Students			Secondary School Students	High School Students
		1st and 2nd grades	3rd and 4th grades	5th and 6th grades		
and obtaining the skills for it	life plan foreseeing the future. • Getting knowledge necessary for making one's own life plan. • Catching the future realistically relating it to life planning and occupational choice.	before buying goods in practicing how to use pocket money.		plan, considering one's future.	based on one's own sense of value. • Thinking about how to build a better life. • Understanding the mechanisms and the functions of loans.	and expenditure. • Understanding the mechanism of loans and thinking about payment methods and interest rates. • Understanding the pension and the social security system. • Understanding the relationship between people's daily life and economic policy and business cycle. • Imagining realistically one's future relating life planning and occupational choice, and thinking about its relationship

		Goals	Primary School Students			Secondary School Students	High School Students
			1st and 2nd grades	3rd and 4th grades	5th and 6th grades		
							with what one wants to be.
Mecha-nisms of economy and finance	Understand-ing the functions of money and finance	• Understanding the roles and functions of money. • Understanding the roles of financial institutions and the functions of central banks. • Understanding the functions of interest rates.	• Understandin g that we have to pay money when we purchase goods or services. • Being able to distinguish various kinds of coins and notes.	• Understanding that we can save money and use it in the future. • Understanding interest rates through depositing at banks or postal offices.	• Understanding various roles of money through one's daily life. • Understanding the basic functions of banks.	• Understanding the roles of money. • Understanding the types and the functions of financial institutions. • Understanding the functions of central banks. • Understanding the function of settlement of banks. • Understanding types, functions, and mechanisms of various cards. • Understanding how interest rates are determined.	• Grasping the roles of money theoretically. • Understanding the diversification of settlement function. • Understanding the direct and indirect finance. • Understanding the functions of interest rates and the reasons of their fluctuations. • Deepening the understanding of the functions of central banks. • Understanding about electronic money and

Goals		Primary School Students			Secondary School Students	High School Students
		1st and 2nd grades	3rd and 4th grades	5th and 6th grades		regional currencies. • Understanding the relationship between financial liberalisation and one's own daily life.
Understanding the mechanism of the economy	• Understanding the role of households, firms and governments and the circulation of goods and money. • Learning the functions of markets and understanding the significance of the market economy. • Understanding the relationship between industry development and the overseas economy.	• Learning that goods and money are exchanged. • Learning that goods have values.	• Examining regional productive activities and understanding how goods and money are circulated,. • Understanding how prices of goods are determined. • Understanding the functions and roles of companies.	• Understanding the circulation of goods and money among households, firms, governments and banks. • Understanding why prices of goods change. • Understanding that firms invest by borrowing money. • Understanding the circulation of goods and money between Japan and	• Understanding the circulation of goods and money among households, firms, financial institutions, the government and foreign countries. • Understanding the significance of market economy. • Understanding their effects on one's daily life and the meaning of yen appreciation and depreciation. • Understanding the functions, roles	• Drawing the overview of circulation of goods, money and people among households, firms, financial institutions, the government and foreign countries. • Understanding the functions of goods markets, financial markets, securities markets and foreign exchange

Goals		Primary School Students			Secondary School Students	High School Students
		1st and 2nd grades	3rd and 4th grades	5th and 6th grades		
				foreign countries.	and social responsibilities of corporations. • Understanding various fund collecting methods firms do.	markets. • Understanding the forming, reasons for being and social functions of firms. • Understanding the globalisation of the economy.
Understanding the fluctuations of economy and the need for economic policy	• Understanding the relationship between business fluctuations, prices, interest rates, and stock prices. • Understanding the monetary policy of central banks and economic policy of the governments. • Understanding how business fluctuations and economic policy are related to one's own life.		• Becoming aware of the relationship between one's own daily life, regional productive activities and the fluctuations of economy.	• Understanding how one's daily life and the society change when the economy fluctuates.	• Understanding the reasons of economic fluctuations. • Understanding the relationship between economic fluctuations and macroeconomic indicators. • Understanding the monetary policy by central banks. • Understanding the package of measures of government to stimulate the	• Arranging and understanding the macro mechanism of economic fluctuations. • Understanding the aims and means of central bank's monetary policy. • Understanding the government's package of measures to stimulate the

Goals		Primary School Students			Secondary School Students	High School Students
		1st and 2nd grades	3rd and 4th grades	5th and 6th grades		
					economy.	economy and the budget deficits.
Understanding various problems in the economy and the role of the government	• Getting interested in the wide-ranging problems that the economy is faced with. • Acquiring the attitude to think rationally and subjectively seeking for the settlement of a problem. • Understanding the role of the government.	• Noticing that people need to pay for using public facilities.	• Understanding various public activities supporting society and the necessary money for them.	• Relating to one's daily life, getting interested in problems occurring in society. • Understanding types of taxes and their significance.	• Obtaining the habit of reading newspapers. • Getting interested in wide-ranging problems in the economy. • Understanding the role of the government through its annual expenditure and revenue.	• Collecting information on the issues of interest and understanding them deeply. • Acquiring the attitude to try to solve problems rationally and subjectively. • Thinking about the policies that the government should take in order to solve the economic and social problems. • Thinking about the effective use of money.

		Goals	Primary School Students			Secondary School Students	High School Students
			1st and 2nd grades	3rd and 4th grades	5th and 6th grades		
Consumer's rights and risks and preventing financial trouble	Obtaining basic skills to enable independent and appropriate decision making and to enable a fruitful life	• Becoming aware of rights and responsibilities of consumers. • Acquiring the attitude of acting as a self-reliant consumer. • Acquiring the skills of gathering information and utilising it accurately.	• Taking care of defective products.	• Becoming aware of the importance of taking safety and environment into consideration in one's life as a consumer.	• Obtaining the ability to make better decisions by utilising information. • Learning the role of consumer centres.	• Understanding basics of contracts. • Learning the consumer's rights and the obligations through reading the Consumer Act. • Understanding the meaning of product liability. • Being able to live one's life as a consumer taking environment and society into consideration.	• Understanding the meaning and the important notice of contracts and the meaning of self responsibility. • Understanding the Consumer Contract Act. • Understanding the protection of personal information. • Obtaining skills to gather information and utilise it for one's life as a consumer.
	Prevent consumer troubles concerning financial transactions and multiple	• Learning the actual situation of financial troubles and multiple debt problems and acquiring the attitude needed to avoid them. • Learning the skills of		• Learning how to deal with troubles and how to consult appropriate institutions.	• Learning the actual situation of financial troubles in which primary school students are involved.	• Learning the important notice of the use of credit cards. • Learning the examples of troubles which	• Learning concrete means to deal with troubles and cultivating skills of practicing them.

125

	Goals	Primary School Students			Secondary School Students	High School Students
		1st and 2nd grades	3rd and 4th grades	5th and 6th grades		
debt problems	dealing with troubles utilising laws and social systems.			• Not borrowing money from friends nor lending it to them.	happened in the use of internet and cellular phones, and understanding how to prevent troubles. • Distinguishing scams and swindles, and learning how to avoid damages from them. • Being able to calculate interest rates and understanding how heavy is the burden to pay interests on loans. • Learning about the cooling-off system. • Knowing the consultant offices to visit when one meets troubles.	• Learning the roles and the functions and the important notice of various cards. • Knowing the present situations of people in multiple debt problems and avoiding easy borrowing. • Realising the relationship between interest rates and loan payments, and understanding the importance of interest rates. • Knowing the consultant offices for people in multiple debt problems and learning how to consult them.

Goals		Primary School Students			Secondary School Students	High School Students
		1st and 2nd grades	3rd and 4th grades	5th and 6th grades		
Becoming sensible consumers	• Understanding the meaning of controlling one's desire and acquiring the attitude to do so in one's daily life. • Acquiring the attitude to think about better ways to deal with money.	• Learning that one cannot have all that he or she wants. • Acquiring the habit to use goods carefully.	• Becoming aware of the importance of moderate life through learning how to use money and practicing it in one's daily life.	• Learning that troubles related to money annoy one's family. • Learning that usage of money varies depending upon individuals.	• Knowing people who live happily with little money and thinking about their sense of values. • Thinking about predecessors' lives and their sense of money through biographies and novels. • Thinking about the relationship among money, accidents and crimes occurring in society.	• Thinking about the relationship between individual's sense of money and what a society should be.

	Goals	Primary School Students			Secondary School Students	High School Students
		1st and 2nd grades	**3rd and 4th grades**	**5th and 6th grades**		
Career education	Understanding the meanings of work and the choice of occupation • Understanding the significance of work and the value of money. • Acquiring the attitude of thinking about one's occupational choice subjectively. • Understanding the rights and obligations of workers.	• Becoming aware of the excellence of workers. • Helping with the housework.	• Understanding the pains of labour and the value of money through participating in educational activities as cultivation.	• Understanding the importance of work and difficulty of getting money. • Understanding that one serves for the society through one's work one. • Getting interested in one's occupation in the future considering one's merits and disadvantages	• Learning the relationship between work and wage. • Realising work through occupational experiences, thinking about future occupation and gathering information about it. • Understanding the significance of work and its role in the society. • Thinking about NEET and part-time workers by choice. • Understanding the rights of workers.	• Thinking concretely about occupational choice through selecting one's career. • Thinking about the occupation one selected and its significance in the society. • Understanding that one's lifetime income depends on one's occupation and is diverse. • Acquiring the attitude to fulfil worker's obligation as well as understanding worker's rights.
	Willingness to live and • Understanding that various efforts are	• Becoming aware of	• Knowing the wishes of	• Understanding dreams, efforts	• Acquiring the attitude of having	• Thinking about means and

	Goals	Primary School Students			Secondary School Students	High School Students
		1st and 2nd grades	3rd and 4th grades	5th and 6th grades		
having vitality	needed to produce added value. • Understanding that the creation of added value is the motive power for the development of economy and society. • Acquiring the attitude to have a dream and to make efforts toward its realisation.	contrivances and efforts of salespersons.	salespersons, and becoming aware of various efforts and contrivances that salespersons make.	and ideas of people and companies in the local community.	dreams and hopes, knowing what is needed to realise them, and acquiring the attitude to make an effort. • Understanding the mechanisms, and the contrivance of and the efforts needed for company management through participation in simulative company formation.	actual steps to realise future dreams, and making necessary efforts. • Thinking about starting a business and thinking over necessary knowledge and practical plans for doing so. • Understanding the means to increase the added value in company management.
Having gratitude for society and being willing to contribute to its improvement	• Understanding that people have various ties with society and cultivating the mind to keep rules and to have gratitude for others. • Cultivating the attitude of thinking about and practicing what one can do for improving the	• Becoming aware of the importance of doing something in co-operation with friends. • Awakening one's roles through	• Cultivating the attitude to be responsible for one's work and to complete it. • Having gratitude and respects for people	• Understanding the importance of working in cooperation with others. • Becoming aware of the significance of working in co-operation with	• Widening one's horizons to objects supporting one's life (parents, societies, foreign countries, natural environments, etc.) and having gratitude for them. • Thinking about	• Viewing better societies and thinking about and practicing what is needed and one should do toward them. • Thinking about what social

Goals	Primary School Students			Secondary School Students	High School Students
	1st and 2nd grades	3rd and 4th grades	5th and 6th grades		
society.	helping housework and doing assigned works in the class. • Becoming aware of the importance of keeping promises.	supporting one's life. • Understanding the importance of keeping rules.	others through non-profit activities (volunteers, etc.). • Being conscious of keeping laws.	various social contributions (to work, to participate in voluntary activities, to donate, etc.) and acquiring the attitude to practice them. • Understanding the relationship between keeping laws and rules, and maintaining public order.	responsibility of firms and what social contribution of enterprises should be, relating them to one's occupational choice. • Understanding that keeping laws and rules is also important for the market economy to work enough.

Appendix 3.A3

The Netherlands: Learning targets*

*   Source: National Institute for Family Finance Information (Nibud), 2013.

Learning goals age 6-8 (lower primary school)

Main theme 1: mapping

Keeping proper accounts

- Not applicable.

Performing transactions

- Children can count money and perform operations with it.

- They can pay small amounts in cash.

- They know what change is and can deal with it.

- They know the various way of paying and the associated concepts, such as cash, getting money from a cash dispenser (ATM) and a debit card.

Earning money of your own

- They know that people work in order to earn money.

Keeping track of income and expenditure

- They know how much money they have.

Main theme 2: responsible spending

Making choices

- They know that not everything is for sale.

- They know that you can make choices with the money you spend.

- They choose for themselves how they want to spend their pocket money or other money.

- They understand that you can spend money only once.

Controlling temptation

- They know that there are advertisements.

- They know that advertisements sometimes make things seem better than they really are.

- They know that there may be advertisements in free video games.

Comparing products and prices

- They know that some products are worth more than others.

- They know that not everything is equally expensive.

Main theme 3: anticipating

Financial planning
- Not applicable.

Saving
- They know what saving is and can say what its advantages are.
- They can save money over short periods for a specific purpose.

Dealing with loans
- Not applicable.

Obtaining insurance
- Not applicable.

Main theme 4: dealing with financial risks

Assessing the financial consequences and risks of events and situations
- They know why it is important to keep money safe.

Assessing the risks and yields of products with financial consequences
- Not applicable.

Main theme 5: having sufficient knowledge (knowing the financial landscape)

Knowing the value of money
- They can recognise the various euro coins and banknotes.
- They can arrange coins and banknotes in order of their value.
- They know that the same amount can be paid in different ways (with different coins and banknotes).
- They know that things cost money.
- They know the function of money and what it is for.
- They know that money has value, and act accordingly (for example, they keep it in a safe place and do not leave it lying around).

Having knowledge of financial concepts and topics
- They can recognise standard symbols relating to money, such as the euro sign (€) and a debit card.

Knowing their rights and duties as consumers and employees
- Not applicable.

Being able to obtain advice and help on money matters
- Not applicable.

Learning goals age 9-11 (upper primary school)

Main theme 1: mapping

Keeping proper accounts

- Children are able to keep important documents (paper or digital).

- They can recognise which documents (paper or digital) are important (certificates, bank statements, identity cards and so on).

Performing transactions

- They can make purchases of their own.

- They can calculate how much change they will get when they make a purchase.

- They know how to pay safely.

- They know that you can also pay by telephone (text message or landline).

Earning money of your own

- They know that you can do odd jobs for payment.

- They know that there are differences in income and that not everyone earns the same amount.

Keeping track of income and expenditure

- They can keep track of what they spend.

Main theme 2: responsible spending

Making choices

- They can adjust their wishes to what they can afford.

- They know that you can spend your money only once.

- They understand that different preferences and priorities lead to different choices.

Controlling temptation

- They know what advertising is and what it is for.

- They can recognise various kinds of advertising, such as advertisements on television and radio, in television programmes, in magazines, in the street and in shops, on the Internet, in apps and social media and in video games.

- They can explain why businesses advertise.

- They understand how and why businesses use social media.

- They understand that businesses offering 'free' things eventually want to/have to make money.

- They understand that businesses therefore make money in other ways than by charging money for the actual product.
- They understand that if you buy branded products you are also paying for the brand name.

Comparing products and prices

- They can arrange products in order of price, from cheap to expensive.
- They can compare prices before making a purchase.
- They can compare prices of products in terms of the same quantity/unit.
- They know that there are cheaper and more expensive versions (different brands) of the same product.
- They understand that different features (of a product) affect people's purchasing choices.
- They understand that if you buy certain products you have to buy additional products before you can use them.

Main theme 3: anticipating

Financial planning

- They can work out how long they will have to save for their intended purpose.

Saving

- They can save money over a longer period for a specific purpose.

Dealing with loans

- They know what borrowing money is.
- They know what borrowing money from a bank is.
- They know what it means to borrow money from other people.

Obtaining insurance

- They know that there are risks (things getting broken, theft, fire and so on) and that these risks have financial consequences.

Main theme 4: dealing with financial risks

Assessing the financial consequences and risks of events and situations

- They know that even if something is offered 'free' there may still be financial consequences attached to it.

Assessing the risks and yields of products with financial consequences

- They know what interest is.

Main theme 5: having sufficient knowledge (knowing the financial landscape)

Knowing the value of money

- They know that the price of a product reflects its value.
- They know the role of money (status and societal values).
- They can assess the value of money and products.
- They can put together a total amount in various ways.

Having knowledge of financial concepts and topics

- They know what the function of a bank is.
- They know the difference between a current account and a savings account.

Knowing their rights and duties as consumers and employees

- Not applicable.

Being able to obtain advice and help on money matters

- Not applicable.

Learning goals age 12-14 (lower secondary school)

Main theme 1: mapping

Keeping proper accounts

- Children can keep important documents (paper or digital) such as contracts, guarantee certificates, bank statements, income statements tidily and find them immediately.
- They can keep log-in data for websites and log-in pages safely.
- They can keep receipts either for guarantees or in order to exchange products.

Performing transactions

- They can make their payments on time.
- They can use a debit card safely.
- They are aware of the potential dangers when using a debit card.
- They can keep PIN numbers and other codes, log-in data and passwords secret.
- They know what to look out for to make sure a website and/or e-mail is safe and trustworthy.
- They are aware of the potential dangers when paying, such as phishing, money mules and skimming.
- They know what online banking is.

Earning money of your own

- They know how to claim back tax if they are employed.

Keeping track of income and expenditure

- They can check their expenditure.

- They can work out how much they spend each month, and what they spend it on.

Main theme 2: responsible spending

Making choices

- They understand the positive and negative consequences of their payment decisions.

- They know the difference between money that has to be spent and money that can be spent.

- They know which expenditure they cannot avoid.

- Before making a purchase, they can work out whether they can afford it.

- They do not spend more money than they have.

- They understand that their social environment affects their choices, and vice versa.

Controlling temptation

- They can recognise advertising, commerce and social pressure.

- They are aware of the impact of advertisements on their spending.

- They are aware of the influence of their friends and classmates on their spending.

- They can distinguish between their own wishes and wishes suggested by advertisements and other people.

- They can assess whether a 'special offer' really is one.

- They can make choices on the basis of what they need and/or already intend to buy, rather than the fact that it is a 'special offer'.

Comparing prices and products

- They can assess the price of a product.

- They can compare various products (or versions of a product) in terms of price and quality.

- They can obtain information (from shops and/or the Internet) before buying a product.

- They know whether a particular product is cheap or expensive compared with similar products on offer elsewhere.

- They can calculate the real overall costs of a purchase, including the purchase price and any associated products or costs.

Main theme 3: anticipating

Financial planning

- When making current purchases, they can take account of greater expenditure that they expect to incur and/or things they want to save money for.

Saving

- They know why it is a good idea to have money in reserve.

- They can save money for longer periods.

- They understand that saving money for something will take a certain amount of time.

Dealing with loans

- They can pay back money they have borrowed.

- They know what a debt is.

- They can say what the difference is between borrowing money and having debts.

- They know that there are various ways of borrowing money.

Obtaining insurance

- They know what insurance is and what it is for.

Main theme 4: dealing with financial risks

Assessing the financial consequences and risks of events and situations

- They know that there are terms and conditions attached to the purchase or use of a product or service (bought in a shop or online) and that these may have financial consequences.

- They can work out what financial consequences are attached to anything offered 'free'.

Assessing the risks and yields of products with financial consequences

- They know the risks involved in lending other people money.

- They understand the consequences of failing to pay back borrowed money.

Main theme 5: having sufficient knowledge (knowing the financial landscape)

Knowing the value of money

- They know that the price of a product is made up of various costs.

- They know that, over time, you cannot always continue to buy the same thing for the same amount of money.

Having knowledge of financial concepts and topics

- Not applicable.

Knowing their rights and duties as consumers and employees

- If they are employed, they know that they and their employers must abide by certain rules.

- They know that there is a minimum wage for young people.

- They know the difference between reported (legal) and unreported (illegal) employment.

- They know what tax is and why you pay it.

Being able to obtain advice and help on money matters

- Not applicable.

Learning goals age 15-17 (upper secondary school)

Main theme 1: mapping

Keeping proper accounts

- Adolescents can keep important documents (paper or digital) tidily without any assistance and on their own initiative.

- They can check their bank balances.

- They can check whether the transactions are correct.

- They can take account of terms of notice.

- They can make use of the information in their accounts, for instance when applying for allowances, submitting tax returns or making payments.

Performing transactions

- They can manage their own bank affairs.

- They can pay their bills on time.

- They can bank online safely.

- They can recognise abnormalities in their bank balances.

- They are aware of the potential dangers when using debit cards and banking online.

- They can check the safety and trustworthiness of websites where they make online purchases.

Earning money of your own

- They can claim back tax if they have been employed.

- They know which factors affect wage levels.

- If they are employed, they can check whether they are being paid at least the minimum wage for young people.

- If they are employed, they are able to find out about legislation on working hours and permitted kinds of work.

- If they are employed, they can find out about the relevant employment conditions and make use of them if the situation calls for it.

Keeping track of income and expenditure

- They can keep track of their income and expenditure.

- They can list their assets and debts.

- They can work out how much they have to/can spend over a given period.

Main theme 2: responsible spending

Making choices

- They can meet their payment obligations.

- They can take account of their payment obligations when spending money on other things.

- They can set priorities in their spending.

- They can decide whether they can afford a particular purchase.

- When making a purchase, they can take account of other expenditure they expect or intend to incur.

- They can adjust their purchasing behaviour to what they can afford.

- They can cut back on their expenditure if they have less money to spend (unexpectedly or otherwise).

- They can adjust their income and expenditure to planned or unplanned changes in their circumstances.

Controlling temptation

- They can withstand advertisements, influence by other people (social pressure) and other temptations.

- If they tend to spend money easily or on an impulse, they know how to control themselves.

- They can see through 'special offers'.

Comparing prices and products

- When purchasing a product or subscription they can calculate the fixed and variable costs and any additional costs (e.g. for administration or dispatch)

- When comparing products and subscriptions they can take account of all the fixed, variable and additional costs.

- When comparing and purchasing products they are able to read and take account of the 'small print' and the terms and conditions.

- When choosing a product or subscription they are able to consider not just the price and the quality, but also the terms and conditions and their own personal situation and wishes.

- They can develop their own criteria for purchasing products.

Main theme 3: anticipating

Financial planning

- They can take account of future expenditure in their current spending.

- They can set short-, medium- and long-term goals and take account of these in their expenditure.

- They know when they will have more or less expenditure (high- or low-expenditure months) and more or less income (high- or low-income months) and can take account of this in their spending.

Saving

- They can set money aside for unexpected costs or necessary expenditure.

- They can periodically set money aside.

Dealing with loans

- They know that you should only borrow money if you know that you can pay back the loan and the interest by the agreed date.

- They know the various ways of borrowing and the differences and similarities between them.

- They are able to consider alternatives to borrowing before deciding to borrow.

- They can name various kinds of debt.

Obtaining insurance

- They know how insurance works.

- They can name various kinds of insurance.

- They know whether a particular kind of insurance is compulsory, necessary, desirable or optional in their own situation.

- They can decide, on the basis of their personal situation and preferences, whether or not to take out a given optional insurance.

Main theme 4: dealing with financial risks

Assessing the financial consequences and risks of events and situations

- They know that changes can occur in the course of their lives (such as living on their own, living with a partner, becoming unemployed, having children or getting divorced) and that these changes can affect their financial situation.
- They can assess and reconsider open-ended subscriptions, and change or end them if necessary.

Assessing the risks and yields of products with financial consequences

- They know how risks and yields are related.
- They can name several ways of increasing assets, and know how these differ in terms of risk and yield.
- They know that when purchasing financial products (savings schemes, insurance, loans and so on) they need to consider not only the costs and yields but also the risks, the contract length and the terms and conditions.
- They are able to assess the short- and long-term financial risks, terms and conditions and costs of a financial or other product before purchasing it.
- They can make choices between saving, insurance and borrowing, based on their personal situation (financial or otherwise) and preferences
- They know the financial and other consequences of having an overdraft, purchasing in instalments, taking out a loan and having a credit card.

Main theme 5: having sufficient knowledge (knowing the financial landscape)

Knowing the value of money

- They know what inflation is and what it implies.
- They know they will have fixed costs if they live on their own.
- They can calculate these fixed costs.
- They can make a realistic assessment of their future income.

Having knowledge of financial concepts and topics

- They know what financial responsibilities and obligations you have when you are 18.
- They are aware of the Dutch student funding system.
- They are aware of how student loans work.
- They know which legislation (on allowances, benefits and insurance) you may have to deal with when you are 18.

Knowing their rights and duties as consumers and employees

- They know the value of, and need for, education and training.

- They know the differences between working for an employer and working for yourself.

- They know what financial arrangements you have to make if you work for yourself.

Being able to obtain advice and help on money matters

- They know which bodies or organisations you can approach if you have certain questions about money.

Appendix 3.A4

New Zealand: Financial capability progressions[*]

---

[*] This new framework will be released online by the Ministry of Education in the course of 2014.

Table 3.A4.1. Learning outcomes

Capability	Theme	Level 1	Level 2	Level 3	Level 4	Level 5	Level 6	Level 7	Level 8
Manage money and income	Money	• Recognise coins and notes. • Describe ways of using money (cash) for different purposes. • Recognise that money has worth, i.e. value.	• Use coins and notes for simple transactions – give and receive change. • Discuss different ways of paying and receiving payment for goods and services, e.g. cash, EFTPOS, bartering. • Discuss the purpose of money, i.e. may be exchanged for items of equal value.	• Use coins and notes for transactions and calculate correct change. • Describe different ways of paying and receiving payment for goods and services e.g. EFTPOS, debit cards. • Describe the purpose of money, e.g. paying for goods, services.	• Recognise the value of New Zealand's currency in relation to currencies of other countries. • Compare different ways of paying and receiving payment for goods and services, e.g. debit cards.	• Convert New Zealand dollars into other currencies (and vice versa) and give examples of when this is useful. • Compare and contrast different ways of paying and receiving payment for goods and services, e.g. debit cards.	• Calculate exchange rates against New Zealand's currency and explain effects changes have on individuals, e.g. planning an overseas holiday. • Describe different ways of transferring money between people and organisations, e.g. Internet banking, debit cards, emerging technologies.	• Calculate exchange rates against New Zealand's currency and explain effects changes have on New Zealand's economy, e.g. imports, exports. • Compare different ways of transferring money between people and organisations, e.g. Internet banking, debit cards, emerging technologies.	• Calculate exchange rates against New Zealand's currency and explain effects changes have on the global economy, e.g. trade, inflation. • Compare and contrast different ways of transferring money between people and organisations, e.g. Internet banking, debit cards, emerging technologies.
	Spending	• Investigate what people "need to" spend money on, e.g. food,	• Explore spending choices for a given amount of money and	• Discuss why individuals/wh ānau may have different spending	• Compare individual spending choices and priorities at	• Compare spending choices and priorities of individuals/wh	• Describe different ways of spending, e.g. online purchasing,	• Describe different views about making wise spending choices in	• Describe and explain different views about making wise spending

Capability / Theme	Level 1	Level 2	Level 3	Level 4	Level 5	Level 6	Level 7	Level 8
	clothing, shelter. • Discuss why and how people make choices about spending money, e.g. when buying food for lunches.	recognise that people's spending choices differ, e.g. food, clothing. • Discuss the concept of getting value for money when spending, e.g. when buying family groceries.	priorities. • Investigate different ways to get value for money when spending, e.g. when buying household items.	different stages of life. • Describe different ways to get value for money when spending, e.g. when buying clothing, toiletries, haircuts. • Discuss external factors that can affect peoples' financial choices, e.g. advertising, peer pressure.	ānau in relation to age, circumstance. • Compare different ways of getting value for money with regard to spending. • Describe external factors that can affect peoples' financial choices, e.g. advertising, peer pressure.	layby, hire-purchase, phone plans. • Explain external factors that can affect peoples' financial choices, e.g. advertising, peer pressure.	relation to age and circumstance. • Explain different ways of spending, e.g. online purchasing, layby, hire-purchase, phone plans. • Describe and explain the effects of inflation on spending.	choices in relation to age and circumstance. • Describe and explain the impact(s) of external factors on spending, e.g. inflation, exchange rates, GST. • Describe and explain different sources of financial advice in relation to wealth creation.
Credit & debt	• Discuss the responsibilities in borrowing and paying back.	• Give examples of using credit to buy goods and services.	• Explain how credit and interest works.	• Describe the cost of credit from different financial institutions. • Discuss differences between "good" and "bad" debt.	• Compare banks and other financial institutions according to interest. • Explain what credit worthiness means for an	• Calculate and compare interest rates charged by banks and other financial institutions. • Describe and explain the relationship	• Demonstrate understandings of interest charged by banks and other financial institutions in relation to amount borrowed,	• Describe and explain interest charged by banks and other financial institutions in relation to amount borrowed,

Capability	Theme	Level 1	Level 2	Level 3	Level 4	Level 5	Level 6	Level 7	Level 8
						individual. • Explore examples of "good" and "bad" debt including manageability of debt and its long term impact, e.g. purpose, use, providers and types of credit, long term, short term debt.	between credit worthiness and the cost of credit, e.g. unsecured vs secured loans, credit rating. • Describe manageable and unmanageable credit and debt, e.g. use of credit, types of credit, interest payment, tax. • Make decisions about incurring "good" and "bad" debt in relation to age, income, and circumstance, e.g. purpose, providers and types of credit, long term, short term debt, interest rates.	interest rate, time and risk. • Identify credit options to manage finances, e.g. credit cards, personal loans. • Describe the future financial responsibilities of utilising tertiary study funding options. • Describe the consequences of making decisions about "good" and "bad" debt in relation to age, income, and circumstance, e.g. purpose, providers and types of credit, long term, short term debt, interest	interest rate, time and risk. • Demonstrate understand-ings of credit for personal financial management, e.g. housing. • Compare and contrast credit options and recommend strategies to manage finances. • Describe and explain the consequences of making decisions about "good" and "bad" debt in relation to age, income, and circum-stance, e.g. purpose, providers and types of credit, short term / long term

Capability	Theme	Level 1	Level 2	Level 3	Level 4	Level 5	Level 6	Level 7	Level 8
	Saving & Investing	• Discuss why and how people save money.	• Identify the benefits of saving money. • Explore simple interest through hands on activities.	• Discuss the concept of getting good returns on savings. • Explain simple interest. • Recognise that peoples' saving choices differ.	• Investigate and evaluate the role of banks. • Calculate simple interest. • Compare differences in saving choices and outcomes between individuals/whānau/groups. • Investigate how varying interest rates affect lenders and borrowers.	• Compare banks and other savings institutions according to risk, interest paid, and access to funds. • Explain and calculate compound interest. • Explore how age, income, and circumstance affect financial decisions. • Investigate different investment products as a way of saving, e.g. KiwiSaver.	• Calculate and compare interest rates, including compounding interest, paid by banks and other financial institutions. • Describe how age, income, and circumstance affect financial decisions, e.g. holidays. • Describe saving and investment options for individuals/whānau/groups, e.g. KiwiSaver, term deposits, bonds, property, shares.	rates. • Describe and explain interest paid by banks and other financial institutions in relation to amount invested, interest rate, time, and risk. • Describe and explain how age, income, and circumstance affect financial decisions, e.g. buying a car. • Calculate and compare inflation rates on the real return of investments. • Describe and explain investment options in relation to age,	debt, interest rates. • Describe and explain interest paid by banks and other financial institutions in relation to amount invested, interest rate, time, and risk. • Describe and explain how age, income, and circumstance affect financial decisions, e.g. tertiary study, donations to charity. • Plan a simple long term personal investment portfolio, e.g. KiwiSaver, workplace savings schemes,

Capability / Theme	Level 1	Level 2	Level 3	Level 4	Level 5	Level 6	Level 7	Level 8
Income & taxation	• Describe ways in which people earn or receive income. • Discuss how having more or less money affects spending choices.	• Identify regular and irregular sources of income, e.g. wages, gifts, prizes. • Discuss how having more or less money affects spending choices for individuals/whānau.	• Explore different sources of income, e.g. interest, wages, salary. • Explore how having more or less money affects spending choices for individuals/whānau/groups/communities.	• Compare differences in income from various sources, e.g. wages, dividends, transfer payments (benefits). • Explain how income contributes to well-being of individuals/whānau/groups. • Discuss why people pay income tax, and how it is collected.	• Investigate the way people get paid including wage and salary deductions. • Make income-related calculations for personal financial management, e.g. hourly, weekly, net pay, annual gross pay. • Compare different rates of taxation commitments. • Describe how taxation contributes to community	• Interpret income-related calculations for personal financial management, e.g. pay slips. • Describe the effect of life-stage factors on personal income sources, e.g. pocket money, job, investments • Perform GST calculations. • Describe different income taxes and deductions and their	income and circumstance, e.g. KiwiSaver, term deposits, bonds, property, shares. • Make an informed decision relating to personal income and explain its consequences, e.g. further education, change of job or career, changes in habits and spending priorities. • Explain the effect of significant events at different life-stages on personal financial income, e.g.	property, sharemarket. • Explain options to increase personal income, e.g. secondary income, promotion, pay increase, unearned income. • Explain the effect of significant events at different life stages on personal financial income, e.g. buying a home, going overseas. • Describe and

3. COMPARING SELECTED FINANCIAL EDUCATION LEARNING FRAMEWORKS

Theme Capability	Level 1	Level 2	Level 3	Level 4	Level 5	Level 6	Level 7	Level 8
					well-being.	impact on income, e.g. personal tax, withholding tax, PAYE. • Explain taxation and other deductions or payments relating to personal income, e.g. KiwiSaver, student loan repayments.	tertiary study, leaving home. • Explain various types of income, and measures of income, e.g. salaries, bonuses, commission, dividends, interest. • Describe and explain how different taxes, e.g. rates, are spent at a local level. • Describe and explain an issue/s around taxation relating to individuals, e.g. duty on international purchases.	explain how different taxes are spent at a national level, e.g. Government budget. • Describe and explain an issue/s around taxation relating to the New Zealand economy.

Capability	Theme	Level 1	Level 2	Level 3	Level 4	Level 5	Level 6	Level 7	Level 8
	Budgeting & financial management	• Give examples of "needs" and "wants".	• Explain simple budget choices that prioritise "needs" and "wants".	• Create a simple budget for an activity or event, prioritising "needs" and "wants". • Use simple money management tools to monitor a given budget, e.g. a spreadsheet. • Identify regular financial commitments whānau have to make.	• Create a budget for a specific activity and timeframe. • Use money management tools, including online and hard copy bank statements, to monitor a given budget. • Identify regular financial commitments individuals/whānau/groups have to make.	• Create an individual/whānau/group budget prioritising "needs" and "wants". • Use financial management tools to monitor a given budget. • Describe life-stage financial event/s and the financial decisions required, e.g. starting secondary school.	• Prepare a budget to manage individual/whā nau/group finances. • Monitor and adjust a given budget to achieve goals. • Describe life-stage financial event/s and the financial decisions required, e.g. getting a part-time job. • Interpret personal financial documents, e.g. statements, accounts.	• Prepare, monitor, and adjust a budget to reflect changing financial circumstances, and achieve goals. • Plan for life-stage financial event/s and make the financial decisions required, e.g. going flatting, getting a job, retiring. • Reconcile personal records with financial documents, e.g. receipts, statements.	• Prepare, monitor, and adjust a budget to reflect changing financial circumstances, and achieve goals. • Plan for life-stage financial event/s and make the financial decisions required, e.g. tertiary study, buying a home, going overseas. • Reconcile personal records with financial documents, query inaccuracies and register complaints.

3. COMPARING SELECTED FINANCIAL EDUCATION LEARNING FRAMEWORKS

Capability	Theme	Level 1	Level 2	Level 3	Level 4	Level 5	Level 6	Level 7	Level 8
Set goals	Setting financial goals and planning ahead	• Identify a short-term money goal and discuss how to attain it.	• Set a financial goal as part of planning a project or activity and identify the steps needed to attain it.	• Create a plan for short term and long term saving based on individual/whānau/group goals.	• Investigate how financial planning can help to attain life goals, e.g. saving for tertiary study. • Discuss different sources of financial advice.	• Describe career choices and the financial goal setting required to attain different options. • Compare and contrast different sources of financial advice.	• Set an individual / whānau / group financial goal and plan its implementation. • Describe and compare different sources of financial advice in relation to wealth creation.	• Set an individual/whānau/group financial goal and plan its implementation. • Demonstrate understandings about wealth creation.	• Develop a plan to achieve long-term financial goal/s. • Demonstrate understandings about wealth creation through personal financial planning.
Manage risk	Identifying and managing risk	• Recognise the importance of keeping money safe. • Describe ways of keeping money safe.	• Discuss the importance of keeping money safe. • Describe ways of keeping money safe.	• Identify types of financial risk for individuals/whānau/groups. • Explain ways of keeping money safe	• Discuss different types of financial risk for individuals/whānau/groups.	• Describe ways of managing risk involved in different investments.	• Compare and contrast risk management strategies for individual / whānau / group finances, e.g. bonds, other financial products. • Describe the role insurance plays in protecting assets, e.g. car, home contents.	• Describe and explain risk and return for individual/whānau/group financial management, e.g. tenancy agreements. • Explain the role different types of insurance play in reducing financial risk.	• Explain risk and return, and diversification for individual/whānau/group financial management. • Investigate the benefits and risks of taking out a student loan.

Capability	Theme	Level 1	Level 2	Level 3	Level 4	Level 5	Level 6	Level 7	Level 8
	Rights and responsibilities	• Recognise the importance of paying for things, e.g. goods.	• Discuss buyers' rights, e.g. returning faulty goods.	• Understand buyers have rights, e.g. warranties.	• Understand that buyers and sellers have rights, e.g. being able to apply for redress. • Discuss different sources of financial advice.	• Understand that buyers and sellers have responsibilities, e.g. Fair Trading Act, banking regulations. • Compare and contrast different sources of financial advice. • Recognise crimes such as identity theft and scams, and identify ways of avoiding them.	• Describe the rights and responsibilities of buyers and sellers, e.g. Consumer Guarantees Act. • Understand legal contracts when purchasing products or services, e.g. hire purchase, phone plans, gym membership contracts. • Describe and compare different sources of financial advice in relation to wealth creation. • Identify trustworthy providers of products and services.	• Explain the rights and responsibilities of buyers and sellers, and how to seek redress, e.g. providing proof, writing a letter. • Interpret legal contracts when purchasing products or services, e.g. hire purchase, phone plans, gym membership contracts. • Describe and compare different sources of financial advice in relation to wealth creation.	• Compare and contrast legal contracts for purchasing products or services, e.g. hire purchase, phone plans, mortgages.

For senior secondary teachers, these achievement objectives, achievement standards, and unit standards may provide, or be adapted to include, contexts or aspects for financial capability teaching.

New Zealand Curriculum

Social Studies

- Understand how individuals, groups, and institutions work to promote social justice and human rights.
- Understand how cultures adapt and change and that this has consequences for society.

- Understand how communities and nations meet their responsibilities and exercise their rights in local, national, and global contexts.
- Understand how conflicts can arise from different cultural beliefs and ideas can be addressed in different ways with differing outcomes.

- Understand how policy changes are influenced by and impact on the rights, roles, and responsibilities of individuals and communities.
- Understand how ideologies shape society and that individuals and groups respond differently to these beliefs.

Economics

- Understand how, as a result of scarcity, consumers, producers, and government make choices that affect New Zealand society.
- Understand how the different sectors of the New Zealand economy are interdependent.

- Understand how economic concepts and models provide a means of analysing contemporary New Zealand issues.
- Understand how government policies and contemporary issues interact.

- Understand that well-functioning markets are efficient but that governments may need to intervene where markets fail to deliver efficient or equitable outcomes.
- Understand how the nature and size of the New Zealand economy is influenced by interacting internal and external factors.

Mathematics and statistics

Number and algebra

- Apply everyday compounding rates.
- Find optimal solutions, using numerical approaches.
- Generalise the properties of operations with rational numbers, including the properties of exponents.
- Relate rate of change to the gradient of a graph.

Mathematics

- Display the graphs of linear and non-linear functions and connect the structure of the functions with their graphs.
- Choose appropriate networks to find optimal solutions.
- Manipulate rational, exponential, and logarithmic algebraic expressions.
- Sketch the graphs of functions and their gradient functions and describe the relationship between these graphs.

Mathematics

- Display and interpret the graphs of functions with the graphs of their inverse and/or reciprocal functions.
- Use permutations and combinations.
- Manipulate complex numbers and present them graphically.

Statistics

• Plan and conduct investigations using the statistical inquiry cycle:
  – justifying the variables and measures used
  – managing sources of variation, including the use of random sampling
  – identifying and communicating features in context (trends, relationships between variables, and differences within and between distributions), using multiple displays
  – making informal inferences about populations from sample data
  – justifying findings, using displays and measures
• Evaluate statistical reports in the media by relating the displays, statistics, processes, and probabilities used to the claims made
• Investigate situations that involve elements of chance:
  – comparing discrete theoretical distributions and experimental distributions, appreciating the role of sample size
  – calculating probabilities in discrete situations
	• Carry out investigations of phenomena, using the statistical inquiry cycle:
	  – conducting surveys that require random sampling techniques, conducting experiments, and using existing data sets
	  – evaluating the choice of measures for variables and the sampling and data collection methods used
	  – using relevant contextual knowledge, exploratory data analysis, and statistical inference
	• Make inferences from surveys and experiments:
	  – making informal predictions, interpolations, and extrapolations
	  – using sample statistics to make point estimates of population parameters
	  – recognising the effect of sample size on the variability of an estimate
	• Evaluate statistically based reports:
	  – interpreting risk and relative risk
	  – identifying sampling and possible non-sampling errors in surveys, including polls
	• Investigate situations that involve elements of chance:
	  – comparing theoretical continuous distributions, such as the normal distribution, with experimental distributions
	  – calculating probabilities, using such tools as two-way tables, tree diagrams, simulations, and technology
		• Carry out investigations of phenomena, using the statistical inquiry cycle:
		  – conducting experiments using experimental design principles, conducting surveys, and using existing data sets
		  – finding, using, and assessing appropriate models (including linear regression for bivariate data and additive models for time-series data), seeking explanations, and making predictions
		  – using informed contextual knowledge, exploratory data analysis, and statistical inference
		  – communicating findings and evaluating all stages of the cycle
		• Make inferences from surveys and experiments:
		  – determining estimates and confidence intervals for means, proportions, and differences, recognising the relevance of the central limit theorem
		  – using methods such as re-sampling or randomisation to assess the strength of evidence
		• Evaluate a wide range of statistically based reports, including surveys and polls, experiments, and observational studies:
		  – critiquing causal-relationship claims
		  – interpreting margins of error
		• Investigate situations that involve elements of chance:
		  – calculating probabilities of independent, combined, and conditional events
		  – calculating and interpreting expected values and standard deviations of discrete random variables
		  – applying distributions such as the Poisson, binomial, and normal

Achievement objectives from the senior secondary teaching and learning guides

Senior Social Studies

6.2 - Understand how cultures adapt and change and that this has consequences for society.

7.1 - Understand how communities and nations meet their responsibilities and exercise their rights in local, national, and global contexts.

7.2 - Understand how conflicts can arise from different cultural beliefs and ideas can be addressed in different ways with differing outcomes.

8.1 - Understand how policy changes are influenced by and impact on the rights, roles, and responsibilities of individuals and communities.

8.2 - Understand how ideologies shape society and that individuals and groups respond differently to these beliefs.

Accounting

6.1 - Manage the financial affairs of individuals, whānau, and local small entities, including community organisations, while acting with integrity.

6.2 - Make use of appropriate communication tools and skills to process, report and interpret financial information for individuals, whānau, and local small entities, including community organisations.

7.1 - Manage the financial affairs of individuals, whānau, and local or regional small or medium entities, including community organisations, that operate accounting sub-systems, while acting with integrity.

7.2 - Make use of appropriate communication tools and skills to process, report and interpret information for individuals, whānau, and local or regional small or medium entities, including community organisations, that operate accounting sub-systems.

8.1 - Manage the financial affairs of individuals, whānau, and small, medium, or large entities, including community organisations, that may be local, regional, national, or global, to enable internal and external users to make effective and ethical decisions.

8.2 - Make use of appropriate communication tools and skills to process, report and interpret information for individuals, whānau, and small, medium, or large entities, including community organisations, that may be local, regional, national, or global.

Business studies

6.1 - Understand how, as a result of internal and external factors, small business owners make operational decisions that have consequences for the success of their business.

6.2 - Plan, carry out, and then review a one-off business activity, basing recommendations for the future on market feedback.

7.1 - Explore how and why large businesses in New Zealand make operational decisions in response to internal and external factors.

7.2 - Plan, take to market, review, and then refine a business activity incorporating a community well-being focus, basing recommendations for the future on market feedback.

8.1 - Analyse how and why New Zealand businesses operating in global markets make operational and strategic decisions in response to interacting internal and external factors.

8.2 - Plan, take to market, review, and then refine and innovative, sustainable business activity; analyse the activity and its success in the market place.

Economics

6.1 - Understand how, as a result of scarcity, consumers, producers, and government make choices that affect New Zealand society.	7.1 - Understand how economic concepts and models provide a means of analysing contemporary New Zealand issues.	8.1 - Understand that well-functioning markets are efficient but that governments may need to intervene where markets fail to deliver efficient or equitable outcomes.
6.2 - Understand how the different sectors of the New Zealand economy are interdependent.	7.2 - Understand how government policies and contemporary issues interact.	8.2 - Understand how the nature and size of the New Zealand economy is influenced by interacting internal and external factors.

Mathematics and statistics

Number and algebra / Mathematics / Mathematics

Number and algebra	Mathematics	Mathematics
6.3 - Apply everyday compounding rates	7.2 - Display the graphs of linear and non-linear functions and connect the structure of the functions with their graphs.	8.2 - Display and interpret the graphs of functions with the graphs of their inverse and/or reciprocal functions.
6.4 - Find optimal solutions, using numerical approaches	7.5 - Choose appropriate networks to find optimal solutions.	8.3 - Use permutations and combinations.
6.6 - Generalise the properties of operations with rational numbers, including the properties of exponents.	7.6 - Manipulate rational, exponential, and logarithmic algebraic expressions.	8.9 - Manipulate complex numbers and present them graphically.
6.8 - Relate rate of change to the gradient of a graph.	7.9 - Sketch the graphs of functions and their gradient functions and describe the relationship between these graphs.	

Statistics

Statistics		
6.1 - Plan and conduct investigations using the statistical inquiry cycle: A – justifying the variables and measures used B – managing sources of variation, including the use of random sampling C – identifying and communicating features in context (trends,	7.1 - Carry out investigations of phenomena, using the statistical inquiry cycle: A – conducting surveys that require random sampling techniques, conducting experiments, and using existing data sets B – evaluating the choice of measures for variables and the sampling and data collection methods used	8.1 - Carry out investigations of phenomena, using the statistical inquiry cycle: A – conducting experiments using experimental design principles, conducting surveys, and using existing data sets B – finding, using, and assessing appropriate models (including linear regression for bivariate data and additive models for time-series data), seeking explanations, and

relationships between variables, and differences within and between distributions), using multiple displays D – making informal inferences about populations from sample data E – justifying findings, using displays and measures 6.2 - Evaluate statistical reports in the media by relating the displays, statistics, processes, and probabilities used to the claims made 6.3 - Investigate situations that involve elements of chance: A – comparing discrete theoretical distributions and experimental distributions, appreciating the role of sample size B – calculating probabilities in discrete situations	C – using relevant contextual knowledge, exploratory data analysis, and statistical inference 7.2 - Make inferences from surveys and experiments: A – making informal predictions, interpolations, and extrapolations B – using sample statistics to make point estimates of population parameters C – recognising the effect of sample size on the variability of an estimate 7.3 - Evaluate statistically based reports: A – interpreting risk and relative risk B – identifying sampling and possible non-sampling errors in surveys, including polls 7.4 - Investigate situations that involve elements of chance: A – comparing theoretical continuous distributions, such as the normal distribution, with experimental distributions B – calculating probabilities, using such tools as two-way tables, tree diagrams, simulations, and technology	making predictions C – using informed contextual knowledge, exploratory data analysis, and statistical inference D – communicating findings and evaluating all stages of the cycle 8.2 - Make inferences from surveys and experiments: A – determining estimates and confidence intervals for means, proportions, and differences, recognising the relevance of the central limit theorem B – using methods such as re-sampling or randomisation to assess the strength of evidence 8.3 - Evaluate a wide range of statistically based reports, including surveys and polls, experiments, and observational studies: A – critiquing causal-relationship claims B – interpreting margins of error 8.4 - Investigate situations that involve elements of chance: A – calculating probabilities of independent, combined, and conditional events B – calculating and interpreting expected values and standard deviations of discrete random variables C – applying distributions such as the Poisson, binomial, and normal

NCEA

Accounting

Level 1	Level 2	Level 3
AS90976 1.1 - Demonstrate understanding of accounting concepts for small entities	AS91174 2.1 - Demonstrate understanding of accounting concepts for an entity that operates accounting subsystems	AS91404 3.1 - Demonstrate understanding of accounting concepts for a New Zealand reporting entity
AS90977 1.2 - Process financial transactions for a small entity	AS91175 2.2 - Demonstrate understanding of accounting processing using accounting software	AS91405 3.2 - Demonstrate understanding of accounting for partnerships
AS90978 1.3 - Prepare financial statements for sole proprietors	AS91176 2.3 - Prepare financial information for an entity that operates accounting subsystems	AS91406 3.3 - Demonstrate understanding of company financial statement preparation
AS91179 2.6 - Demonstrate understanding of an accounts receivable subsystem for an entity	AS91177 2.4 - Interpret accounting information for entities that operate accounting subsystems	AS91407 3.4 - Prepare a report for an external user that interprets the annual report of a New Zealand reporting entity
AS90980 1.5 - Interpret accounting information for sole proprietors	AS91179 2.6 - Demonstrate understanding of an accounts receivable subsystem for an entity	AS91408 3.5 - Demonstrate understanding of management accounting to inform decision-making
AS90981 1.6 - Make a financial decision for an individual or group	AS91386 2.7 - Demonstrate understanding of an inventory subsystem for an entity	AS91409 3.6 - Demonstrate understanding of a job cost subsystem for an entity
AS90982 1.7 - Demonstrate understanding of cash management for a small entity	AS91481 2.5 - Demonstrate understanding of a contemporary accounting issue for decision making	
AS91386 2.7 - Demonstrate understanding of an inventory subsystem for an entity		

Business studies

Level 1	Level 2	Level 3
AS90837 1.1 - Demonstrate an understanding of internal features of a small business	AS90843 2.1 - Demonstrate understanding of the internal operations of a large business	AS91379 3.1 - Demonstrate understanding of how internal factors interact within a business that operates in a global context
AS90838	AS90844	AS91380

1.2 - Demonstrate an understanding of external factors influencing a small business	2.2 - Demonstrate understanding of how a large business responds to external factors	3.2 - Demonstrate understanding of strategic response to external factors by a business that operates in a global context
AS90839 1.3 - Apply business knowledge to an operational problem(s) in a given small business context	AS90845 2.3 - Apply business knowledge to a critical problem(s) in a given large business context	AS91381 3.3 - Apply business knowledge to address a complex problem(s) in a given global business context
AS90840 1.4 - Apply the marketing mix to a new or existing product	AS90846 2.4 - Conduct market research for a new or existing product	AS91382 3.4 - Develop a marketing plan for a new or existing product
AS90841 1.5 - Investigate aspects of human resource processes in a business	AS90847 2.5 - Investigate the application of motivation theory in a business	AS91383 3.5 - Analyse a human resource issue affecting businesses
AS90842 1.6 - Carry out and review a product-based business activity within a classroom context with direction	AS90848 2.6 - Carry out, review and refine a business activity within a community context with guidance	AS91384 3.6 - Carry out, with consultation, an innovative and sustainable business activity
		AS91385 3.7 - Investigate the exporting potential of a New Zealand business in a market, with consultation

Senior Social Studies

AS91039 1.1 - Describe how cultures change	AS91279 2.1 - Demonstrate understanding of conflict(s) arising from different cultural beliefs and ideas	AS91596 3.1 - Demonstrate understanding of ideological responses to an issue(s)
AS91040 1.2 - Conduct a social inquiry	AS91280 2.2 - Conduct a reflective social inquiry	AS91597 3.2 - Conduct a critical social inquiry
AS91041 1.3 - Describe consequences of cultural change(s)	AS91281 2.3 - Describe how cultural conflict(s) can be addressed	AS91598 3.3 - Demonstrate understanding of how ideologies shape society

Economics

AS90983 1.1 - Demonstrate understanding of consumer choices, using scarcity and/or demand	AS91222 2.1 - Analyse inflation using economic concepts and models	AS91399 3.1 - Demonstrate understanding of the efficiency of market equilibrium
AS90984 1.2 - Demonstrate understanding of decisions a	AS91223 2.2 - Analyse international trade using economic	AS91400 3.2 - Demonstrate understanding of the efficiency of

3. COMPARING SELECTED FINANCIAL EDUCATION LEARNING FRAMEWORKS

producer makes about production	concepts and models	different market structures using marginal analysis
AS90985 1.3 Demonstrate understanding of producer choices using supply	AS91224 2.3 - Analyse economic growth using economic concepts and models	AS91401 3.3 - Demonstrate understanding of micro-economic concepts
AS90986 1.4 - Demonstrate understanding of how consumer, producer and/or government choices affect society using market equilibrium	AS91225 2.4 - Analyse unemployment using economic concepts and models	AS91402 3.4 - Demonstrate understanding of government interventions to correct market failures
AS90987 1.5 - Demonstrate understanding of a government choice where affected groups have different viewpoints	AS91226 2.5 - Analyse statistical data relating to two contemporary economic issues	AS91403 3.5 - Demonstrate understanding of macro-economic influences on the New Zealand economy
AS90988 1.6 - Demonstrate understanding of the interdependence of sectors of the New Zealand economy	AS91227 2.6 - Analyse how government policies and contemporary economic issues interact	
	AS91228 2.7 - Analyse a contemporary economic issue of special interest using economic concepts and models	

NQF – Personal financial management

US24701 - Demonstrate an introductory knowledge of credit for personal financial management.	US24703 - Demonstrate and apply knowledge of credit for personal financial management.
US24702 - Demonstrate knowledge of credit for personal financial management.	US24708 - Set a complex personal financial goal and plan its implementation.
US24707 - Set a personal financial goal and plan its implementation.	
US25242 - Demonstrate knowledge of wealth creation through the personal financial planning process.	
US25246 - Demonstrate an introductory knowledge of risk and return for personal financial management.	US25247 - Demonstrate knowledge of risk and return, and diversification for personal financial management.
US24699 - Make an informed decision relating to personal income and evaluate its consequences.	US1874 - Prepare IRD employer reporting documentation for PAYE, FBT and GST.
US24697 - Perform income-related calculations for personal financial management.	
	US24696 - Demonstrate knowledge of personal income, credit, and taxation, and the impact of

	employment decisions on them.
	US20078 - Describe taxation, financial, and insurance responsibilities for small business owner-operators.
US24704 - Demonstrate knowledge of banking products and services for personal financial management.	
US24705 - Interpret and verify accuracy of personal financial documents.	US18956 - Demonstrate knowledge of financial management for an entity.
US24695 - Demonstrate knowledge of income, taxation, and other deductions for personal financial management.	
US24709 - Produce a balanced budget for an individual.	US24710 - Produce a balanced budget for a family or household.

Service Industries Pathway - NCEA achievement standards recommends as vocational pathways for financial manager, financial adviser, financial dealer

http://youthguarantee.net.nz/assets/Uploads/MOE-VP-Services-RD2-final3.pdf

Accounting

AS90976 1.1 - Demonstrate understanding of accounting concepts for small entities	AS91174 2.1 - Demonstrate understanding of accounting concepts for an entity that operates accounting subsystems
AS90977 1.2 - Process financial transactions for a small entity	AS91175 2.2 - Demonstrate understanding of accounting processing using accounting software
AS90978 1.3 – Prepare financial statements for sole proprietors	
AS90979 1.4 - Prepare financial information for a community organisation's annual general meeting	
AS90980 1.5 - Interpret accounting information for sole proprietors	
AS90981 1.6 - Make a financial decision for an individual or group	
AS90982	

1.7 - Demonstrate understanding of cash management for a small entity

Business Studies

AS90837
1.1 - Demonstrate an understanding of internal features of a small business

AS90838
1.2 - Demonstrate an understanding of external factors influencing a small business

AS90840
1.4 - Apply the marketing mix to a new or existing product

AS90843
2.1 - Demonstrate an understanding of internal operations of a large business

AS90844
2.2 - Demonstrate understanding of how a large business responds to external factors

AS90846
2.4 - Conduct market research for a new or existing product

AS90847
2.5 - Investigate the application of motivation theory in a business

Economics

AS91222
2.1 - Analyse inflation using economic concepts and models

AS91223
2.2 - Analyse international trade using economic concepts and models

AS91224
2.3 - Analyse economic growth using economic concepts and models

AS91226
2.5 - Analyse statistical data relating to two contemporary economic issues

AS91227
2.6 - Analyse how government policies and contemporary economic issues interact

AS91228
2.7 - Analyse a contemporary economic issue of special interest using economic concepts and models

Annex A

INFE Guidelines for Financial Education in Schools[*]

This annex reproduces the INFE Guidelines for Financial Education in Schools. The Guidelines are aimed at providing high-level non-binding international guidance to assist policy makers and interested stakeholders in designing, introducing and implementing efficient financial education programmes in schools. They are complemented by the Guidance on Learning Frameworks, defined as planned and coherent approaches to financial education in the formal school sector that define overall learning outcomes or standards for financial education.

---

[*] The Guidelines and accompanying Guidance were developed and finalised through a comprehensive consultative process which involved a very wide range of stakeholders. The OECD International Network for Financial Education (INFE) elaborated and then approved the Guidelines and Guidance for further consultation in October 2010. In April 2011, they were approved by the Committee on Financial Markets (CMF) and Insurance and Private Pensions Committee (IPPC) (the two committees in charge of the financial education project) for public consultation, which took place in August-September 2011. The revised versions of the Guidelines and Guidance were approved by the INFE in October 2011; and the final versions as well as the present INFE Guidelines were approved by the CMF and the IPPC on 1 March 2012 and also circulated to the OECD Education Policy Committee. At their August 2012 meeting, Ministers of Finance of the Asia-Pacific Economic Cooperation (APEC) supported the Guidelines and encouraged their implementation in APEC economies.

Background

These Guidelines and accompanying Guidance on Learning Frameworks on Financial Education built on preliminary research conducted by the OECD Committee on Financial Markets in 2008 and an international survey carried out through the OECD/INFE in 2009/2011 as well as analytical reports to be published by the OECD in 2012.

The Guidelines and accompanying Guidance were developed and finalised through a comprehensive consultative process between 2010 and 2012. This process involved a wide range of stakeholders: They were originally developed by the OECD/INFE though a dedicated group of experts, submitted to a public consultation on the OECD website and reviewed and approved by the OECD Legal Department and OECD bodies in charge of financial education (the Committee on Financial Markets and the Insurance and Private Pensions Committee) in March/April 2012. The Guidelines have also been supported by Asia-Pacific Economic Cooperation Ministers of Finance at their August 2012 meeting and their implementation has been encouraged in APEC economies (APEC, 2012).

The process for the development of these Guidelines has also provided valuable inputs for the work on the international option on financial literacy of the OECD Programme for International Student Assessment (PISA) 2012 exercise. In particular, the development of the framework for the assessment has largely been drawn from the Guidelines, accompanying Guidance and background material.

The INFE Guidelines and accompanying Guidance stand as a tailored supplement to the OECD/INFE High-Level Principles on National Strategies for Financial Education and the OECD 2005 Recommendation. They provide high-level, non-binding international guidance and frameworks to assist policy makers and interested stakeholders in designing, introducing and implementing efficient financial education programmes in schools.

The Guidelines are aimed at addressing the challenges linked to the introduction of financial education in schools. They can be adapted as necessary to national, regional or local circumstances and in particular, to different curricula and the diversity of education systems. Depending on the structure of education systems at the different geographical levels, the Guidelines apply to school programmes starting in kindergarten until the end of formal schooling as needed.

The term "financial education in schools" is used in these Guidelines to refer to the teaching of financial knowledge, understanding, skills, behaviours, attitudes and values which will enable students to make savvy and effective financial decisions in their daily life and when they become adults. Financial literacy (or capability) is used to refer to the intended outcomes of the educational programmes.

INFE Guidelines for Financial Education in Schools

Framework for the integration of financial education into school curricula

Financial education in school programmes: an integral part of national coordinated strategies

Financial education should ideally be integrated into the school curriculum as part of a co-ordinated national strategy for financial education involving the wider community. School programmes should allow every child in a country or jurisdiction to be exposed to this subject matter through the school curriculum. The introduction of financial education should be preceded by, and based on, an assessment and analysis of the status and level of financial education provided through existing curricula and the current level of financial literacy of children and young people.

The identification of a public leader or co-ordinating body at national level should ensure the relevance and long-term sustainability of the programme. This could be a Government Ministry, such as Finance or Education, a financial regulator, a central bank or a committee/council gathering several public authorities. Whichever co-ordinating body is chosen, it is essential to secure the involvement and support of the Ministry of Education and of the education system at national, regional and local levels, preferably from the beginning of the project (see also Box 1.1).

Appropriate, tailored and quantifiable goals

The overarching goals of the introduction of financial education in the school curriculum should be set through the nationally coordinated strategy and based on relevant education principles. More detailed objectives and outputs should preferably be established in dedicated learning frameworks[1] on financial education. Such learning frameworks should preferably be endorsed by the public educational authorities.

The content of the learning framework may vary according to national, regional or local circumstances, the identification of particular talents, needs, aspirations and gaps, the structure and requirements of the education system, and cultural or religious considerations, as well as the approach adopted for the introduction of financial education in schools. In this respect, in some countries or jurisdictions, learning frameworks on financial education may need to be developed at regional or local level.

Learning frameworks on financial education should ideally encompass knowledge and understanding; skills and behaviours; as well as attitudes and values. These may also encompass entrepreneurial skills. In general, learning frameworks on financial education in schools provide some guidance either to schools and teachers or to local authorities on:

- Learning outcomes.
- Topic/content of financial education classes which can include, according to school age/grade:
  - Money and transactions;
  - Planning and managing finances;

- – Risk and rewards; and,

- – Financial landscape.

- • Pedagogical approaches and methods.

- • Resources:

  - – Number of hours per week and/or per year depending on school grade;

  - – Time span in the curriculum.

- • Assessment and monitoring criteria.

Flexible implementation

The introduction of financial education in schools should ideally involve a flexible approach and be adaptable to national, regional and/or local circumstances.

It is often preferable for financial education to be introduced as a mandatory and statutory component of the national curriculum in order to ensure it is actually taught to all children through their time at school.

The introduction of financial education as a stand-alone subject or module would in principle ensure that sufficient time and resources were devoted to its teaching. However, considering the constraints on most education systems, the inclusion of financial education in some specific subjects (e.g., mathematics, economics or social sciences, home economics, citizenship, literature or history) or as a horizontal subject integrated in a wider range of classes can also be effective.

Indeed, the inclusion of financial education through a cross-curricular approach may overcome the difficulties posed by overloaded curricula, and allow for the development of more diverse and potentially innovative and engaging ways to link financial literacy to more familiar topics for teachers and students. If this approach is used, it will be important to develop mechanisms to monitor the actual teaching of financial literacy. It will also require the identification, within the dedicated learning framework on financial education, of specific links with other subjects and to provide teachers in the relevant classes with case studies and examples.

Financial education in schools should start as early as possible (ideally in kindergarten and primary schools) and last at least until the end of the formal curriculum and, to the extent possible, the end of high school. The learning framework will have to be adapted to age/grade with the objective of developing sound financial competencies throughout students' time at school.

Box A1.1. Education systems' involvement and support

The involvement of the education system and of the Ministry of Education with the objective of the inclusion of financial education in schools should be encouraged and promoted by interested policy stakeholders (which may be other parts of the government and/or public financial regulatory and supervisory bodies and/or Central Banks) in various ways.

First, depending on national circumstances, stakeholders should, to the extent possible, try to take advantage of "teachable moments' when the population and the education system may be more easily convinced of the importance of financial skills and knowledge for individuals' well-being. The aftermath of the financial crisis has established, albeit in an unfortunate manner, the conditions for the emergence of such awareness in the population in many countries or jurisdictions and throughout national/regional/local education systems. The recent period clearly stands as a unique opportunity to develop long-term programmes and partnerships in this field.

Another method is to develop evidence of need, through the development of surveys on the level of financial literacy and skills of youth in order to bring to the attention of the public and educationalists the gaps and needs of young generations in this critical field. The development of international indicators and benchmarks on financial literacy (including through the inclusion of financial literacy assessment in the OECD Programme for International Students Assessment – PISA) will also represent a compelling tool.

Considering the lack of resources, time and possibly expertise of education systems (which are usually relatively unfamiliar with financial issues as a learning topic), interested public stakeholders may wish to consider directly supporting the development of the financial education curriculum in schools. In this respect, they can seek to provide appropriate solutions to identified constraints of the system and help establishing long-term and flexible roadmap and objectives. For instance, public financial authorities could:

- promote the introduction of financial education in the curriculum through a graduated approach: they could first suggest integrating the subject as a voluntary one, and then, where feasible, as a mandatory horizontal topic in other courses. This approach may be effective where the introduction of financial education as a stand-alone and/or mandatory subject is expected to foster stiff resistance and lead to delays in its implementation;

- assist in the development of a financial education learning framework, taking into account the requirements of the education system;

- support the development and provision of materials to teachers as well as dedicated training; and/or,

- develop concrete partnerships with the Ministry of Education or the education system possibly through Memoranda of Understanding in order to ensure the actual involvement of key education stakeholders as well as establish clear responsibilities, goals, outputs and timescales.

The development of internationally recognised OECD guidelines and recommendations could also provide a powerful argument for policy actions in this area.

Suitability and sustainability of resources

Appropriate, commensurate and long-term financial and in-kind resources should be identified to ensure the sustainability and credibility of the development and implementation of a learning framework on financial education in schools. Such resources can come from public or private sources as long as suitable mechanisms are in place to ensure the objectivity and quality of programmes (see also Box 1.2). In this respect, private funding or in-kind involvement can be sought to secure sufficient financial support and to benefit from the financial expertise of private stakeholders.

**Box A1.2. Managing possible conflicts of interest relating
to private financing and involvement in financial education in schools**

Several means can be considered and established to monitor private funding and manage possible conflicts of interest with the commercial activities of financial institutions involved in financial education in schools:

- Public authorities or independent not-for-profit institutions (such as self-regulatory bodies) can channel and monitor the use of private funding;

- Private funding can be combined with public money;

- In-kind private resources (such as the provision of materials, the development and organisation of training or the intervention of private volunteers in the classroom) should, as far as possible, be the subject of certification (quality marks) or accreditation by public authorities or an independent not-for-profit organisation;

- Rules and standards can be developed to ensure the objectivity of private initiatives in a school context (e.g., avoidance of the use of logos and brands); and,

- Any direct intervention of private volunteers in the classroom should be conducted under the close oversight of teachers and/or the education system's management at large.

Monitoring of progress and impact

Methods and criteria to evaluate the progress and impact of financial education programmes in schools and the efficiency of the different approaches should be planned and established at the outset of the programme. These should preferably involve the monitoring of each stage of the programme's implementation and the quantitative and qualitative measurement of short-term outcomes and long-term impacts in order to improve its efficiency and the accountability of involved stakeholders over time.

In order to ensure the relevance and efficiency of programmes, pilot exercises involving the introduction of financial education in a smaller number of schools or at regional/local level can be considered before spreading the experience on a broader scale.

Various monitoring and evaluation processes can also be put in place including:

1. Monitoring of programmes' implementation and process assessment:

   – Monitoring/evaluation of the actual teaching of financial education in schools (through oversight mechanisms at local, regional and/or national level and case studies);

   – Evaluation of the relevance and impact of programmes, learning framework, related material, and teacher training on financial education. Such evaluation can be based on the collection of feedback from relevant stakeholders in the process (e.g., teachers, education systems management, school leaders, trainers, students, parents and the community); and,

   – Evaluation of students' competencies in financial literacy throughout the curriculum via appropriate assessment tasks in the classroom on a regular basis, formal examinations or through ad hoc national contests.

2. Impact evaluation in the longer term:

    –   Inclusion of financial education in examinations at the end of the formal school curriculum;

    –   Establishment of baseline surveys on the level of financial literacy and skills of students (covering assessment of financial knowledge, understanding, skills, behaviour, attitudes and values), to set a benchmark and establish gaps and needs. These surveys should ideally be repeated at regular time intervals (e.g. 3/5 years) to measure progress over time; and,

    –   Participation in, and use of, available international survey results on the level of financial literacy of students such as the PISA exercises starting in 2012.

Ensuring a suitable involvement of important key stakeholders

In order to be effective, financial education in schools should be integrated into wider community, national and/or regional initiatives. It also requires the commitment and involvement of a potentially vast range of stakeholders from diverse horizons: government, financial regulatory bodies, central banks, education systems, teachers, parents, the community and students should be involved. It may also be relevant and appropriate to seek the commitment of private financial institutions, business leaders and experts from non-for-profit associations, local networks and international organisations.

The role of each stakeholder and extent of involvement will vary depending on national circumstances, education systems and culture. However, the definition of each stakeholder's responsibility and accountability in the process should preferably be established at the outset of the project. Key and central functions should be fulfilled by a central coordinating body (usually composed of public authorities), with the support of the education system, teachers, parents and the community as well as students.

Government, public authorities and education system: a leading and coordinating role

The Government and in particular, the Ministry of Education and other public authorities (such as financial regulatory and/or supervisory authorities and Central Banks) have a leading role to play in:

*   assessing needs and gaps;

*   mapping and evaluating existing initiatives;

*   raising awareness of the importance of financial education in schools;

*   defining the education framework and standards for financial education;

*   leading and providing guidance on the introduction of financial education in schools and best practice models;

*   framing the overall structure of the programme: setting responsibilities, monitoring the process and evaluating intermediate and final results; and,

*   co-ordinating the actions of other stakeholders and overseeing the implementation phase.

The education system, its key local stakeholders and management at various levels, including school level, should be closely involved.

Appropriate mechanisms should be in place to make sure these actors are directly engaged in:

- the promotion of the successful inclusion of financial education in schools; and,

- the elaboration and identification of the best and most efficient ways and tools to meet this goal (including the development of relevant pedagogical methods).

Teachers and school staff; parents and the community; students: a pivotal role

Owing to their pedagogical expertise and close relation to students, teachers should be at the centre of the introduction of financial education in schools. Particular efforts should be made to involve teachers at all stages of the process, convince them of the importance of financial literacy for students and themselves, as well as to provide them with the necessary resources and training so that they feel confident teaching financial literacy in classes.

If external experts and volunteers are engaged in the classroom, teachers should preferably also be involved in, and monitor their work.

Parents and the local community should also be closely engaged, possibly through dedicated programmes and initiatives.

Incentives and signals should in particular be designed to ensure that parents and the community, as well as students, are aware of the importance of financial education for individuals' financial and general well-being and successful interaction with, and inclusion in, society and economic life (see also Section III).

School leaders, such as school principals and executive staff, can also play an instrumental role in efficiently promoting financial education amongst teachers, students and their parents, relatives and the wider community.

Other stakeholders

Other stakeholders such as the business/financial sector, expert consultants and not-for-profit institutions can also play a role in financial education in schools.

Financial institutions directly, or through national associations, can be involved in the introduction of financial education in schools. For instance, they can provide in-kind expertise or financial support for the development of materials, training for teachers or volunteers to interact with students in the classroom. However, this involvement should be clearly separated from their commercial activities and closely monitored and managed to prevent any possible conflict of interest (see Box 1.2).

Consulting firms or not-for-profit institutions with special expertise in the area may also be involved, for example in the development of school materials (building on the learning framework) or in training for teachers.

International organisations such as the OECD, in particular through the International Network on Financial Education (INFE), also have a role in providing international guidance and (in-kind) support and tools to the efficient development of financial education in schools.

Top-down and bottom-up approach

The involvement of all interested stakeholders, especially those in the education system, should preferably be secured through both a top down and a bottom up approach. In this respect, the development of memoranda of understanding between concerned partners may be considered to facilitate the smooth and efficient implementation of the programme, and to ensure clear accountabilities.

Designing and promoting efficient means and methods

Adequate supporting tools and means should be identified, devised and made available to key stakeholders in the education system to facilitate the efficient introduction of financial education in schools.

Appropriate information and training of teachers and other school staff

Appropriate training should be made available to ensure that teachers and other relevant school staff (such as school leaders) are adequately equipped and feel confident and competent in building students' financial competencies.

Such training should be put in place for all teachers who may be in a position to deal with financial education in the classroom either as a stand-alone subject or through other topics (e.g., mathematics, economics, social sciences, home economics, citizenship, literature or history). It should take place as part of the initial teacher training/education (that is, a pre-service course before entering the classroom as a fully qualified teacher), and carried on regularly as part of teachers' continuous professional development.

The main goals of this training should encompass:

- raising teachers' awareness on the importance of financial education in lifelong learning;
- providing them with pedagogical methods to use available teaching resources; and,
- developing teachers' own financial literacy.

Such training should be provided by qualified staff following predefined guidance. Trainers for teachers should in particular possess a sound knowledge of the education system, the requirements of the financial education learning framework, and of efficient pedagogical tools and resources on financial education. If such trainers do not exist, priority should be given to developing the skills of the trainers.

Availability and provision of high quality, objective and effective tools

Availability of, and easy access to, high quality, objective and efficient material and pedagogical methods should be secured and actively promoted with a view to offer teachers the best resources on financial education.

In order to do so, it may be necessary, in some countries or jurisdictions, for government or relevant public bodies to:

- map and assess the quality of available materials and resources such as books, brochures, guides, on-line tools, case studies, games, surveys and pedagogical methods; and,
- select most relevant tools and material to be provided to teachers and schools.

In others, it may be necessary to develop such resources from scratch.

In both cases, criteria and principles for the identification and development of suitable tools should be established (see Box 1.3). Financial education resources made available in a country or a jurisdiction should be assessed by a governmental or independent body according to these criteria. Such a body should preferably introduce a special quality mark or accreditation acknowledging resources matching these criteria.

The appropriate resources should then be made easily accessible to schools and teachers possibly, through a single trusted source or through relevant public authorities (e.g., government, financial regulators; well-known and public or independent website; education system; local network, etc.).

A single source (or maybe several sources) can act as a clearing house on financial education materials available for the classroom. A central source should thus be well organised, and contain clear signposting in order to allow the easy identification of materials and tools according to age, grade, contents and learning outcomes to be achieved.

A central source should also be actively promoted to teachers so that they are aware of the existence of this support and know how to access it.

Box A1.3. Criteria for identification and development of suitable resources on financial education

With a view to efficiently embedding financial education in schools, related resources and pedagogical methods should preferably encompass the following characteristics:

- be in line with the requirements of the national/regional/local learning framework on financial education, and with any national curriculum guidelines of the country or jurisdiction;

- be adapted to students according to their age, talents, needs, aspirations and background; be culturally and gender inclusive and evolved following the school curriculum;

- be relevant for students, taking into account their interests and potential access/use of financial products;

- emphasise the benefits of financial literacy for students' future well-being;

- be objective and marketing free (e.g., avoiding the use of financial firms' logos and promotion of particular financial products);

- be of high-quality, diversified, engaging and attractive for students, using real-world contexts, case studies, inquiry/activity-based learning and problem solving approaches or community-based activities directly involving students (e.g., through simulation, games and interaction with the concrete world);

- make use of the benefits of cross-curricular approaches where relevant (e.g., taking advantage of the possibility to include financial education in diverse subjects);

- involve the monitoring of progress and the quantification of impact on students throughout the curriculum and at its end (through examinations); and,

- be trialled to evaluate their relevance and efficiency with teachers, parents and the community as well as students.

Promotion of appropriate incentives

In order to encourage deeper involvement and motivation of teachers and students in financial education programmes, appropriate incentives can be put in place, such as:

1. Recognising achievements through:

   – Regular examination of students in order to monitor progress;

   – Setting community and national outcome goals in order to evaluate performance;

   – Organisation of special school, local, regional or national contests with the granting of awards and prizes.

2. Making financial matters more visible and attractive through:

   – Organisation of special events on financial education (e.g. 'money' or 'saving' days/weeks) with the participation of well-known community stakeholders;

   – Designing teachers' training on financial education so that they perceive it as a component of their personal development and as a way to improve their own financial well-being; and,

   – Similarly, focusing the teaching of financial literacy in schools on the (immediate) positive outcomes for students, their parents and the community.

Exchange and promotion of international good practices

The development of internationally recognised guidelines and practices and strengthening of policy dialogue and co-operation on the exchange of good practices are also instrumental to the efficient and successful introduction and implementation of financial education in schools. Such guidelines can help policy makers and involved stakeholders in designing and successfully implementing their own strategy on financial education in schools building on, and tapping into, relevant experiences and internationally recognised good practices.

Guidance on learning frameworks on financial education

Definition

A definition of the overall objective for financial education programmes is the first main component of related learning frameworks. In most cases, depending on countries' or jurisdictions' culture, this is referred to as either financial capability or financial literacy, but basically involves a similar content.

Such definition encompasses the competencies that students need to develop in order to make effective and responsible financial decisions in their daily life and when they become adults. Competencies cover financial knowledge, understanding, skills, attitudes and behaviours and the ability to use these effectively.

The definition may focus solely on the personal use and management of money and the impacts of financial decisions on the lives of individuals or it may include a broader perspective that takes account of the interaction between personal financial decision-making and wider society and environment.

Purpose and goals of the framework

Purpose

A financial education learning framework is defined as a planned and coherent approach to financial education in the formal school sector at the national, regional or local level. A financial education learning framework should operate at a meta-level, providing overall learning outcomes or standards for financial education. The framework can then be implemented at the national, regional, local, school or classroom level in the way that is most appropriate for the context.

The framework should begin by explaining its purpose, including:

- Who developed the framework and the development process;
- When the framework was developed;
- The overall aims of the framework;
- How the framework supports the achievement of national, regional or local curriculum objectives;
- Whether the framework has been endorsed and, if so, by whom.

Providing the framework on a web-based platform enables easy access and distribution and for links to be made to relevant supporting information such as teaching resources, assessment tools and relevant curricular materials.

Goals

The overall goals and objectives of the framework should be reflected in a more detailed description of the dimensions of financial literacy. These may include a description of the specific outcomes that students are expected to develop and that will be covered by the financial education programme. The following dimensions can be considered and included:

- Knowledge and understanding;
- Skills and competencies;
- Behaviours;
- Attitudes and values;
- Entrepreneurship.

The descriptions of each of these dimensions should reflect the focus on personal and/or collective aspects needed to be consistent with the definition of financial literacy in the framework.

These descriptions are important in developing teachers' understanding of financial literacy.

Learning outcomes/standards

The framework should provide a description of the desired learning outcomes. These should be related to each of the dimensions of financial literacy.

Outcomes may be statements of the overall outcomes for each of the dimensions or they may be shown as a learning progression across years or curriculum levels. The latter shows the way that the specific dimensions of financial literacy are progressively developed as students move through their schooling career.

Approach to inclusion of financial education in the curriculum

The framework should describe the overall approach to the inclusion of financial education in the curriculum. This should be consistent with the overall approach to the curriculum.

In countries or jurisdictions where national curriculum objectives are outlined but schools have considerable discretion as to how these are implemented at the local level, financial education will not easily be introduced as a compulsory component. The framework may describe how financial education supports the achievement of national curriculum objectives and provide guidance as to how financial education can be integrated into existing subjects or a cross-curricular approach taken. In a cross-curricular approach, financial education is recommended as an engaging and real-world context in which other curricular objectives can be achieved alongside financial education objectives.

In countries or jurisdictions where a more centralised approach is taken, financial education may be mandatory. There is a range of ways for this to occur including as a stand-alone subject; as an explicit module or component of one or more subjects; or integrated into relevant subjects at the school's or teachers' discretion. If an integrated approach is used, it is important to provide specific links between the financial education learning outcomes and the learning outcomes for specific subjects.

The financial education learning outcomes should be linked to over-arching national curriculum objectives, as well as to the learning outcomes for specific subjects.

The framework should describe the year levels or curriculum levels in which financial education should be taught. This may be across the compulsory school sector or it may focus on the levels where it aligns most closely with the curriculum objectives at that level, for example, senior secondary school.

Content and length of courses

The framework generally provides a list of suggested topics. These should not solely be based on developing knowledge and understanding but should also enable students to explore and develop values, attitudes, skills and behaviours.

Where financial education is mandatory or explicitly included as a stand-alone subject or as a module of a subject, the length of the course should preferably be explicitly stated. In other cases, the amount of teaching time given to financial education is not stated.

The framework generally describes the recommended or suggested content for financial education. These should be related to the overall outcomes described in the definition, and the dimensions of financial education set out in the learning framework.

The framework generally provides a list of topics, themes or issues that can be included in the financial education programme. These may be linked to specific subject areas or they may be presented in a way that can be incorporated in a range of subject areas. Topics that are most commonly included in financial education learning frameworks are:

- money and transaction;

- planning and managing finances (including saving and spending; credit and debt; financial decision-making);

- risk and rewards;

- financial landscape (including consumer rights and responsibilities and understanding of the wider financial, economic and social system).

The topics should be relevant to the concerns of students at specific year levels but, at the same time, recognise that financial education needs to prepare students for adult life.

Resources and pedagogical tools

The framework can also provide guidance about the teaching methods that are most effective in developing financial literacy. These may include a description of the overall recommended approach such as using real-world, relevant examples, or inquiry-based learning. Teaching methods should not be solely focussed on developing knowledge but they should provide engaging contexts in which students can develop skills, attitudes and behaviours. Opportunities for students to practice their skills and develop behaviours in authentic and engaging contexts should be recommended and examples provided. Interactive and experiential learning opportunities are recommended.

As well as classroom-based learning, suggestions for learning outside of the classroom such as through extra-curricular activities can be provided.

The framework can provide case studies of the ways that schools and teachers have effectively taught financial education.

The framework should also preferably provide recommended teaching and learning resources and guidance about selecting effective resources. Guidance should be provided about quality assurance indicators and ways to avoid materials that are biased or contain marketing information.

Professional development for teachers and administrators can be provided by the relevant authority in support of the financial education framework and to develop teachers' capability to teach financial education. In some cases, the private sector or not-for-profit organisations may offer professional development, teaching and learning materials and/or volunteers who may be available to visit classrooms. Guidance should be given in the framework about ways to avoid conflicts of interest and to ensure that suitably qualified and, in some cases, approved providers are selected by schools.

Assessment of students' learning in financial education

The framework should provide guidance about appropriate methods for assessing financial education learning outcomes. This should be consistent with approaches to assessment in other areas of learning and for the year level of the student. It is recommended that assessment of skills is included as well as assessment of knowledge and understanding. Assessment involving students in problem-solving and real-world contexts are recommended so they have the opportunity to demonstrate their competencies. Examples of assessment activities may be provided.

Examination of students' achievement should be considered whenever possible. If so, the examination process and criteria need to be outlined in the framework. This includes information on the levels at which students will be examined and whether there will be a stand-alone examination for financial education or whether it will be included in the examination of the relevant subjects. In some cases, formal recognition of student achievement in financial education can be provided by certificates, qualifications or credentials.

Monitoring and evaluation

Monitoring of the framework can occur at the local school level or at the national or regional level.

At the school level, the framework can provide guidance to administrators and teachers to support the planning and implementation of the financial education framework. This includes ways to monitor the outcomes of the financial education programme and the extent to which it is being progressively and consistently implemented across the school at the appropriate levels. This is of particular importance where financial education is not mandated and where schools and teachers are given discretion about how they incorporate financial education outcomes into their teaching programmes. In countries or jurisdictions where external agencies review schools, it may be appropriate to include a review of financial education provision and outcomes in relation to the financial education framework.

At the national or regional level, the implementation and outcomes of the financial education framework should be evaluated. This may be an independent evaluation that can be used to inform the development and implementation of the framework. An evaluation will provide evidence of the effectiveness of the framework in achieving the desired outcomes in terms of increasing financial literacy.

Note

1.   See also the following section: Guidance on learning frameworks on financial education.

References

OECD Recommendations
available at www.financial-education.org

OECD (2005), Recommendation on Principles and Good Practices on Financial Education and Awareness, http://www.oecd.org/finance/financial-education/35108560.pdf

OECD (2008a), Recommendation on Good Practices for Financial Education relating to Private Pensions, http://www.oecd.org/pensions/private-pensions/40537843.pdf

OECD (2008b), Recommendation on Good Practices for Enhanced Risk Awareness and Education on Insurance Issues, http://www.oecd.org/pensions/insurance/40537762.pdf

OECD (2009), Recommendation on Good Practices on Financial Education and Awareness relating to Credit, http://www.oecd.org/finance/insurance/46193051.pdf

OECD/INFE instruments and relevant outputs

APEC (2012), Finance Ministers Policy Statement on Financial Literacy and Education, http://www.apec.org/Meeting-Papers/Ministerial-Statements/Finance/2012_finance/annex.aspx

Atkinson, A. and F-A Messy, (2012), Measuring Financial Literacy: Results of the OECD/INFE Pilot Study, *OECD Working Papers on Finance, Insurance and Private Pensions,* No. 15, OECD Publishing, http://dx.doi.org/10.1787/5k9csfs90fr4-en

Grifoni, A. and F-A Messy, (2012), Current Status of National Strategies for Financial Education: a Comparative Analysis and Relevant Practices, *Working Papers on Finance, Insurance and Private Pensions,* No. 16, OECD Publishing, http://dx.doi.org/10.1787/5k9bcwct7xmn-en

OECD/INFE (2009), Financial Education and the Crisis: Policy Paper and Guidance. available at *www.oecd.org/finance/financial-education/50264221.pdf*

INFE (2010a), Guide to Evaluating Financial Education Programmes, available at *www.financial-education.org.*

INFE (2010b), Detailed Guide to Evaluating Financial Education Programmes, available at *www.financial-education.*org.

INFE (2010)11, Supplementary questions: Additional, optional survey questions to complement the OECD/INFE Financial Literacy Core Questions, available at *www.financial-education.org.*

INFE (2011), High-level Principles for the Evaluation of Financial Education Programmes, available at *www.financial-education.org.*

OECD/INFE (2012), High-level Principles on National Strategy for Financial Education, available at: www.oecd.org/finance/financialeducation/OECD_INFE_High_Level_Principles_National_Strategies_Financial_Education_APEC.pdf

OECD (2013), "Financial Literacy Framework", in OECD, PISA 2012 Assessment and Analytical Framework: Mathematics, Reading, Science, Problem Solving and Financial Literacy, OECD Publishing. doi: 10.1787/9789264190511-7-en

OECD/INFE (2013), Toolkit to Measure Financial Literacy and Inclusion: *Guidance, Core Questionnaire and Supplementary Questions.* Available at *www.financial-education.org.*

ORGANISATION FOR ECONOMIC CO-OPERATION AND DEVELOPMENT

The OECD is a unique forum where governments work together to address the economic, social and environmental challenges of globalisation. The OECD is also at the forefront of efforts to understand and to help governments respond to new developments and concerns, such as corporate governance, the information economy and the challenges of an ageing population. The Organisation provides a setting where governments can compare policy experiences, seek answers to common problems, identify good practice and work to co-ordinate domestic and international policies.

The OECD member countries are: Australia, Austria, Belgium, Canada, Chile, the Czech Republic, Denmark, Estonia, Finland, France, Germany, Greece, Hungary, Iceland, Ireland, Israel, Italy, Japan, Korea, Luxembourg, Mexico, the Netherlands, New Zealand, Norway, Poland, Portugal, the Slovak Republic, Slovenia, Spain, Sweden, Switzerland, Turkey, the United Kingdom and the United States. The European Union takes part in the work of the OECD.

OECD Publishing disseminates widely the results of the Organisation's statistics gathering and research on economic, social and environmental issues, as well as the conventions, guidelines and standards agreed by its members.

OECD PUBLISHING, 2, rue André-Pascal, 75775 PARIS CEDEX 16
(21 2012 02 1 P) ISBN 978-92-64-17481-8 – No. 60007 2014-01

DATE DUE

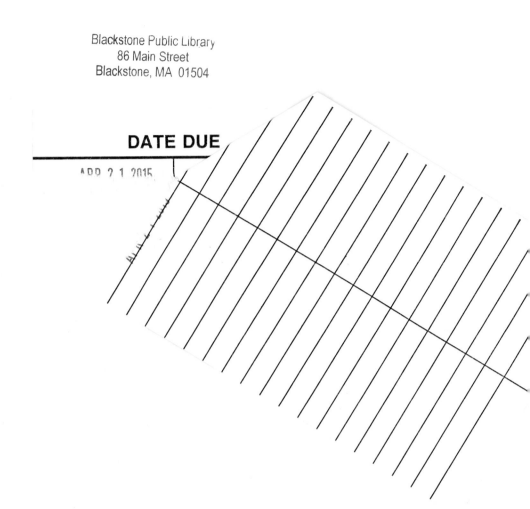

CPSIA information can be obtained at www.ICGtesting.com
Printed in the USA
LVOW01s1604291014

411095LV00001B/25/P

9 789264 174818